The Eastern Mediterranean Lands in the Period of the Crusades

The Eastern Mediterranean Lands in the Period of the Crusades

Edited by P. M. HOLT

ARIS & PHILLIPS LTD., Warminster, England.

ISBN 0 85668 091 5

Distributed in the USA and Canada by
International Scholarly Book Services Inc.,
P.O. Box 555, Forest Grove, Oregon 97116, USA

Printed in England by Biddles Ltd., Guildford, Surrey

CONTENTS

INTRODUCTION

On the eve of the French Revolution, Edward Gibbon published the sixth volume of *The decline and fall of the Roman Empire* which contains the two chapters he devoted to the Crusades and the Frankish states in the Levant, ending with the celebrated and melancholy words, 'a mournful silence prevailed along the coast which had so long resounded with the WORLD'S DEBATE'.[1] Since then the Crusades have become the subject of more specialised scholarly interest, as the abundant and increasing mass of publications bears witness. There is, however, a criticism which may be made of much of Western historical writing on the Crusades, and which has been put clearly by a contemporary scholar:-

"C'est un tableau fort déséquilibré que présente la recherche historique sur les Croisades. Bien qu'il s'agisse là d'une lutte entre Orient et Occident, on a généralement concentré les études sur l'une des deux forces en présence, l'occidentale, laissant l'autre partie comme une sorte de toile de fond, somme toute assez vague et mal comprise."[2]

This lack of balance results from two factors. The first of these is the relative inaccessibility of the oriental sources, particularly to Western historians. The literary sources - chronicles, encomia, biographical dictionaries, chancery manuals - are only slowly being edited and published; archival materials in the true sense (as distinct from documents transcribed in isolation in the literary sources) are almost completely lacking. Translations into Western languages are sparse and uneven in quality and reliability. Secondly, and in consequence of this, the modern historiography of the Islamic Near East in this period is markedly smaller in quantity than (and sometimes also inferior in quality to) the modern historiography of medieval Europe, from which writing on the Crusades has largely developed. So although some important topics have been examined in depth, there are enormous tracts even of political history (to say nothing of institutional and social history) which have not yet been adequately surveyed. To take one example: the Ayyubid period was of critical importance in the dealings of the Frankish states and the neighbouring Muslim powers, while the relations among the members of the Ayyubid clan itself were an important factor in the history of the Near East. Yet apart from Saladin himself, who has been the subject of several biographies (not all displaying outstanding critical acumen), only one Ayyubid ruler has received the detailed attention of an historian.[3] One may remark in passing that the Mamluk sultans, who finally accomplished the overthrow of the Frankish states, have been even more poorly served. Neither al-Ẓāhir Baybars nor al-Manṣūr Qalāwūn has found a biographer, although Götz Schregle's monograph on the brief and transitional career of Shajar al-Durr is a model for anyone who would undertake such studies.[4]

The resonance of Gibbon's closing sentence may lull our critical ears, but in fact it contains two assumptions, both of which deserve some consideration. The first of these is that after the extinction of the Latin kingdom in 1291 'a mournful silence prevailed along the coast'; the second that the episode which then closed had been in some sense 'the WORLD'S DEBATE'. Both assumptions may be queried, and it is worthwhile to do so, since the Gibbonian rhetoric has, consciously or unconsciously, affected much Western thinking about the Crusades. That 'a mournful silence prevailed along the coast' is only partly and briefly true. Certainly it is generally true that, as they were retaken during the Muslim reconquest, the coastal towns were devastated and the castles of the littoral slighted in order to deny a bridgehead to Crusaders from Europe. For the expelled Franks, and for the titular kings of Jerusalem, gazing eastwards from Cyprus, this was no doubt a mournful prospect. The hinterland also suffered from the campaigns of the reconquest and from Mongol invasions in 1259-60 and 1281, although it was far from desolate since, apart from the indigenous inhabitants, warrior tribes of Turcomans, Kurds and even refugee Mongols were settled there for strategic reasons. Once the danger from the Franks and the Mongols had passed, and the Mamluk sultanate had established a firm and centralised control over Syria (such as had never existed in the Ayyubid period), the international trade of the Levant recovered. The colonies of Italian merchants increased, both in the former Frankish ports of Beirut, Tripoli, Acre and Tyre, and in the great inland cities which had always remained under Muslim rule, so that the fifteenth century has been described as 'the apogee of the medieval Levant trade'.[5] The traveller on the Syro-Palestinian coast during the Mamluk sultanate was less likely to experience a mournful silence than the chaffering in several languages of Muslim and Christian merchants of various nationalities.

To what extent, next, were the Crusades 'the WORLD'S DEBATE' - the dispute between Christendom and its great adversary , *Dār al-Islām*? How far were the Christians and Muslims of the time aware of the Crusades as a special and a central episode in the long history of their relations? Modern scholars have stressed a difference of outlook here between the two groups. Thus, Francesco Gabrieli, discussing the Arabic historiography of the Crusades, remarks, 'The Muslims never reached the point, one would say, of regarding the Christian attack in the West as anything fundamentally different from the other wars against the Infidels, whether they were Franks or Byzantines: in Syria itself in the course of the tenth century and before, in Andalus throughout the Spanish Reconquista, in Sicily against the Normans.'[6] A similar point has been made by Claude Cahen, who comments, 'The very term *ḥurūb al-ṣalībiyya*, used to designate them [i.e. the Crusades] in modern Arabic literature, was unknown to ancient authors, ... and seems to have made its appearance during the Ottoman period in Christian circles of the East influenced by French culture.'[7]

These views are perhaps not wholly convincing. The argument from terminology should not be pressed too far. *Al-ḥurūb al-ṣalībiyya* is admittedly an Arabic rendering of 'crusades', but 'crusade' is itself a neologism of the eighteenth century. In the crusading period itself, although there was a late and rarely used Latin term, the usual terms lack a specific content *(expeditio)* or imply the older institution of pilgrimage *(iter in terram sanctam, peregrinatio)*. Perhaps it would be true to say that at first (in Hans Eberhard Mayer's words), 'The line between crusade and pilgrimage was obviously a blurred one',[8] but that as time went on the growing body of historical writing to which the Crusades and the Frankish states gave rise began to confer on them a distinctive character in the eyes of contemporaries. A somewhat similar development seems to have taken place among the Muslims, although the indications of it are not to be found to any great extent in their historical writing. Certainly the First Crusade did not make any wide general impression on *Dār al-Islām* beyond the territories which were actually occupied or immediately threatened. Certainly also the Crusades were seen in the traditional framework of a world polarised between two hostile communities, *Dār al-Islām* and *Dār al-ḥarb*. Certainly too the First Crusade was linked with the setbacks to Islam in Sicily and Spain. There was however a growing recognition that the Crusaders, above all in their occupation of the holy city of Jerusalem, were different from other invaders of *Dār al-Islām*, even from the Byzantines, with whom they were at first confused.[9] To find evidence of Muslim consciousness of the Crusades as a unique episode, one must turn chiefly to the literature composed during the period to encourage and justify the *jihād*, the holy war against the infidel interlopers into the Syro-Palestinian portion of *Dār al-Islām*.

The articles in this volume were originally presented in a seminar held early in 1975 at the School of Oriental and African Studies in London with the aim of bringing together historians working on medieval Europe and the Islamic Near East. The interchange of ideas was undoubtedly profitable to both groups, and it is hoped that these articles will contribute to a further recognition of the common ground between medievalists and orientalists in the methods and content of Crusading historiography. The collection opens with an article by Professor Rosalind Hill on 'The Christian view of the Muslims at the time of the First Crusade'.

Drawing largley on the information provided by the anonymous Norman author of *Gesta Francorum*, she presents the opinions held by the early Crusaders of the beliefs and practices of the Muslims whom they encountered in battle. To the history of medieval Christian polemic against Islam, the contribution of the Anonymous is of an unusual and interesting kind. Unlike most of the controversialists, he was neither a scholar nor a theologian - indeed he was only incidentally a controversialist. He was not particularly well-informed about what Muslims believed, or even what Christian polemicists said they believed, but for that very reason his account is the more enlightening as to the mentality and outlook of the founders of the Frankish states.

Two aspects of the history of those states are dealt with in the articles by Dr. Riley-Smith on 'The survival in Latin Palestine of Muslim administration' and by Dr. Smail on 'The international status of the Latin kingdom'. Dr. Riley-Smith's article serves as a warning against any assumption that the establishment of the Latin kingdom involved a complete break in the institutional and administrative history of the territory it occupied. Had this been so, it would perhaps have been a unique phenomenon. Dr. Riley-Smith summarises his findings in a field which is poorly documented, but which would repay further research. Dr. Smail draws our attention to some unusual features of the Latin kingdom, arising from what was virtually its international character. Its possession of the holiest Christian shrines, the frequent general appeals by the papacy for a crusade, the attempts by the Latin kings themselves to win the support of Western rulers, even by accepting their suzerainty - all these matters subtly change the perspective in which one views the political history of the Latin kingdom, and bring to notice an underestimated factor in medieval European history.

The three following articles deal with the Muslim regime which finally overcame the Crusaders and extinguished the Latin kingdom, the Mamluk sultanate in Egypt and Syria. To Western historians (and to modern Near Eastern historians, habituated to Western concepts) the Mamluk sultanate has usually appeared as paradoxical, anarchic and stagnant: paradoxical, because most of the sultans were brought as slaves into the lands which they later ruled; anarchic, because of the recurrent succession-crises and frequent revolts by over-mighty subjects; stagnant, because the secondary sources give an impression of unchanging institutions and monotonous political developments. Here is not the place to consider this presentation in detail, but a case may be made for the view that Mamluk slavery was essentially a means of procuring the selective and controlled immigration of non-Muslim 'barbarian' warriors into the Islamic lands. Much of the anarchy of the period (which was not as general or as damaging as the secondary sources suggest) arose from the incorporation of this military and ruling group, drawn from outer 'barbarians', in an ancient Islamic society. Finally, the evidence of the chroniclers (rather than that of the chancery handbooks, which have chiefly been exploited for data on the administration) shows institutions which were fluid and developing throughout the two and a half centuries of the sultanate's duration, and a political history which mirrored considerable changes in the internal and external factors affecting the state.

Three aspects of the Mamluk sultanate are studied in these articles. The present writer's 'The structure of government in the Mamluk sultanate' examines the functions of the sultan, the great officers of state and the royal household, and outlines some developments in the period under consideration. Mr. Irwin, in '*Iqṭāʿ* and the end of the Crusader states', considers a fiscal institution of major importance in Islamic history, the *iqṭāʿ*, a term sometimes rendered 'fief' and one which covered as wide a range of practices as did the feudal fief, although the two ranges were not identical and were the products of different historical developments. Mr. Irwin's article is concerned with the *iqṭāʿ* in Syria and Palestine in the late thirteenth century, and raises a number of interesting questions, not least of them the possibility that here we have a meeting-place between Muslim and Frankish institutions. The continuity indicated in Dr. Riley-Smith's article may thus perhaps be traced still further. Dr. Haldane's article, 'Scenes of daily life from Mamluk miniatures', introduces us to a very different field, and reminds us that the autocracy of the Mamluk sultans, the factionalism of the magnates, and the frequent warfare coincided with a high degree of patronage of the arts. The painters, it is interesting to note, responded to the circumstances of their time by the 'Far Eastern' faces they depicted, and the rigid composition reflecting the hierarchic society of the Mamluk sultanate.

Dr. Edbury's article on 'The crusading policy of King Peter I of Cyprus (1359-1369)' forms an appropriate epilogue. Over seventy years after the fall of the Latin kingdom, Peter I, titular king of Jerusalem, led a crusading expedition to the coast of Egypt, sacked Alexandria, and occupied the city for a few days - an event which forms the subject (or the principal subject) of the labyrinthine and diffuse work by al-Nuwayrī al-Iskandarānī.[10] Dr. Edbury sets this episode in the context of the king's policy throughout his reign, and suggests that his aim was not the traditional goal of regaining Jerusalem by conquest or negotiation, but the strengthening of the economic position of Cyprus, whether by holding or by eliminating the great Egyptian port. In spite of King Peter's seeking Western help, and in spite of the pope's authorisation of the expedition, the age of the Crusades had passed into an age of conflict for the mercantile and naval domination of the eastern Mediterranean.

P. M. HOLT

1. Edward Gibbon, *The history of the decline and fall of the Roman Empire* (ed. J. B. Bury), London, 1898, VI, 365. The original date of publication of the volume was 1788.

2. Emmanuel Sivan, *L'Islam et la croisade*, Paris, 1968, 5.

3. Hans L. Gottschalk, *Al-Malik al-Kāmil von Egypten und seine Zeit*, Wiesbaden, 1958.

4. Götz Schregle, *Die Sultanin von Ägypten*, Wiesbaden, 1961.

5. E. Ashtor, 'Profits from trade with the Levant in the fifteenth century', *Bulletin of the School of Oriental and African Studies*, London, xxxviii/2, 1975, 250.

6. Francesco Gabrieli, 'The Arabic historiography of the Crusades', in Bernard Lewis and P. M. Holt (edd.), *Historians of the Middle East*, London, 1962, 98.

7. C. Cahen, CRUSADES, in *Encyclopaedia of Islam* (2nd edn.), II, 64. Cf. E. Sivan, 'Modern Arab historiography of the Crusades', *Asian and African Studies*, Jerusalem, 8/2, 1972, 109-10.

8. Hans Eberhard Mayer, *The Crusades* (tr. John Gillingham), London, 1972, 15.

9. An early stage of this is exemplified in the tract by al-Sulamī, *Kitāb al-jihād* (1105), studied by E. Sivan, 'La genèse de la contre-croisade; un traité damasquin du début du XIIe siècle', *Journal Asiatique*, 1966, 197-224. Material on the further developments is provided in his *L'Islam et la croisade*, but the view that all this amounts to a contemporary Muslim recognition of the distinctiveness of the Crusades is my own.

10. Muḥammad b. Qāsim b. Muḥammad al-Nuwayrī al-Iskandarānī, *Kitāb al-ilmām*, (edd. Etienne Combe and Aziz Surial Atiyya), Hyderabad, 1968-70.

The Christian view of the Muslims at the time of the First Crusade

This paper is in no sense intended to be a study of Islam, or even of Islamic institutions, at the time of the First Crusade, for this would be a vast subject and one which I am quite incapable of tackling. Nor are any of those disrespectful views of the Prophet and his faith, which I am bound to put forward in the course of my argument, to be attributed to me. I am concerned to see him, and the peoples who accepted his teaching, through the eyes of Western Christians of the eleventh and twelfth centuries, all of whom disapproved of him, and some of whom were fully prepared to lose their lives for the recovery of the Holy Sepulchre. People at war do not stand upon the niceties of convention: they are, understandably, inclined to credit even the best of their enemies with horns and a tail. It is with an appreciation of these facts in mind that we must consider the impression of Muslim life and faith which emerges from the works of the historians of the First Crusade.

Western accounts of this crusade fall into two main groups. The first includes men who were actively engaged in the crusade, men such as the unknown author of the *Gesta Francorum*, Raymond of Agiles and Fulcher of Chartres. Together with these we may classify such later historians as William of Tyre, who, though he was born too late to take part in the crusade, had at least an extensive knowledge of the local conditions in which it had been fought, while his acquaintance with the Arabic tongue enabled him to study the Islamic world at first hand. The second group of historians consists of scholars who wrote from hearsay, or who re-hashed the work of first-hand authorities. They lived in western Europe and had no practical experience of the Near East. These men, such as Albert of Aix, Guibert of Nogent, Robert the Monk and Ralph of Caen, had of necessity to draw heavily upon the written works of actual crusaders and especially upon the *Gesta Francorum*. As onlookers, they may at times have seen more of the game than did any one man actively engaged in it, and one of them, Guibert of Nogent, attempted to give a theological explanation of the origin and doctrines of Islam, - an explanation which would have been quite beyond the capabilities of the author of the *Gesta*. Nevertheless they had never met a Muslim, and they knew nothing at first hand of local conditions. This failure to understand local problems, whether of diplomacy or of terrain, could impart a disastrous slant to a man's whole understanding of the crusade, as the Latin settlers in Outremer were to learn to their cost.

The author of the *Gesta* had the advantage, unique among the historians of the First Crusade, of being himself a fighting man. Unlike Fulcher of Chartres and Raymond of Agiles, who were clerics, he was not cut off from the shock of battle; he fought with Muslims and probably killed some of them. He seems to have joined the crusade for two quite simple reasons, a belief (which he shared with the author of the Song of Roland) that 'pagans are wrong, and Christians are right', and the desire to fulfil the feudal contract which bound him to his immediate lord, Bohemond. When, after the taking of Antioch, his two loyalties came into conflict, he chose the first, but he chose it, I think, in some distress of mind. He had no feeling for political advantage or for the founding of a Norman principality in Antioch. He simply wanted to rescue the Holy Sepulchre.

The authority of the *Gesta Francorum*, therefore, is of unique importance. And it is clear that the author, however much he might disapprove of any religion which was not Christian and Catholic, respected Turks at least as worthy opponents on the battlefield. He tells us:-

> 'They have a saying that they are of common stock with the Franks, and that no men, except the Franks and themselves, are naturally born to be knights. This is true, and nobody can deny it, that if only they had stood firm in the faith of Christ and holy Christendom ... you could not find stronger or braver or more skilful soldiers; and yet by God's grace they were defeated by our men.'[1]

The *amīr* to whom Kerbogha committed the defence of the citadel of Antioch was, according to this author, 'honourable and brave',[2] while Kerbogha himself, although credited with pride, ferocity and bombastic boastfulness, is never depicted as a mean or unworthy adversary. He fights fairly, taking no advantage of sorcery, and he promises to any Christians who will deny their faith and join the Turks that 'you shall all be knights, as we are, and we will count you always among our dearest friends'.[3]

It seems probable that this idea of the knightly status of the Turks arose from the fact that they, unlike the Arabs or the Egyptians, made use of cavalry in battle. The author of the *Gesta* had a much lower opinion of the Egyptian troops whom he encountered at Ascalon, who were more careful of their water-flasks than of their weapons, and 'stood about blinded and bewildered ... some in their panic climbed up trees, hoping to hide ... others threw themselves flat on the ground ... so our men slaughtered them as one slaughters beasts in a shambles'.[4] The contrast with battles fought against the Turks is clear. Something of the chivalrous attitude shown in the *Gesta* towards enemies recognised as 'bonny fighters' penetrated back from the front line even to those historians who wrote in the west. Baudri of Dol observes that 'the Saracens are crafty, intelligent and warlike, but alas, alienated from God'.[5] The relation of feudal equality which was assumed to exist between Christian and Muslim 'knights' made it possible, later, for some mixed marriages to take place between the two peoples. Fulcher of Chartres suggests that it was not unusual for Frankish men who settled in the east to take Saracen brides (although of course they insisted on baptism as the pre-requisite of marriage),[6] Richard I seriously proposed that his sister should become the wife of Saladin's brother,[7] and the list of Saracen heroines who appear in the romances of Western Europe continues to the delightful (and improbably-named) Susie Pye, who rescued Lord Beichan from her father's dungeon, followed him to Scotland, and subsequently married him under the baptismal name of Lady Joan.[8]

Relations between Christian and Muslim were not, therefore, embittered, although, reasonably enough, they were antagonistic. After all, if as a Christian you were trying to rescue the Holy Sepulchre and the Muslims held it, you naturally killed as many of them as you could, and counted their deaths as nothing but gain. Each side showed extreme ignorance about the religious beliefs of its opponents, and each seems to have regarded the other as being in some sense polytheistic. The Franks take it for granted that Muslims when in trouble invoke 'the names of their gods',[9] while Ibn al-Qalānisī, author of the *Damascus Chronicle*, refers to the Trinitarian Christians as 'polytheists'.[10] Rather surprisingly, each side also regarded the other as being habitually given to idolatry. There was indeed some reason for the austere Muslim to look askance upon some of the more superstitious forms of devotion bestowed upon crucifixes and ikons, and especially upon wonder-working relics, among the crusaders, but it seems exceedingly odd to find Christian chroniclers solemnly reporting the presence of idols in Muslim mosques - a subject to which I shall return.

Guibert of Nogent is the only western historian of the crusades who attempts to give any theological explanation of Islam, although it is clear that several Christian writers realised the depth of antagonism which lay between the Sunnites and Shiʿites. (William of Tyre, who spoke Arabic and probably talked to ambassadors from Egypt, knew something about the Messianic hope of the Shiʿites, observing that they are not so far removed from the true Christian faith as are other Muslims). Guibert, who was interested in theology, seems to regard Islam as an extreme form of Christian heresy, derived mainly from Arianism. It is worthy of note that he calls Muslims *perfidi* rather than *pagani*, implying by this that they were traitors to the faith, who had been given the chance to see the light of the Christian revelation and had rejected it. He adds that the blame for this lies mainly with the wicked Greek Orthodox priests with whom they came into contact, - men so lost to a sense of all proper devotion that they did not scruple to wait even until after the mid-day meal before consecrating the Eucharist.[11]

Mahomet, according to Guibert, was a heresiarch who believed in the Father alone, disregarding the Holy Ghost and relegating the

Son to a position of mere humanity. He enjoined upon his followers the rite of circumcision, and allowed them otherwise to do as they pleased. In this way he became a *diaboli fistula*, a pipe on which the Devil could play his own tune. Desiring to prove to his followers the divine origin of the Qur'ān, he bound the book to the horns of a certain tame cow, and concealed her in his tent. When in the presence of a great multitude of his followers, he called her by name, she came out and appeared to present him with the book. Seeing this, his followers were persuaded, rather oddly, that he had received it from an angel, and they accepted it as the law of God, binding upon all believers. To punish him for this deception Mahomet came to a bad end, as Guibert records with evident satisfaction. Falling one day into an attack of epilepsy, he was torn to pieces and devoured by pigs, so that nothing was left of him except his heels. This, says Guibert, explains why his followers have ever since that day entirely refused to eat any pork.[12]

Most other Christian writers regard the Muslims not as heretics *(perfidi)* but rather as heathens *(pagani, infideles* or *gentiles)*,[13] although they have no clear-cut picture of what Islam implied. The author of the *Gesta Francorum*, who had no theological knowledge beyond that of an intelligent layman, was clearly a little uncertain as to the distinction between a heathen and a heretic, although he was quite sure that both of them were bad. He included among his *pagani* the Paulicians, who had nothing to do with Islam and are usually classified as Manichaean heretics.[14] Fulcher of Chartres referred to Muslims as being, quite literally, possessed by the Devils, calling them *'gens ancilla daemonibus'*.[15]

This assumption did not prevent some Christian writers, like the author of the *Gesta* himself, from accepting the fact that Muslims, in common with other *pagani*, were capable of practising the cardinal, as opposed to the theological, virtues. Guibert of Nogent tells us the story of how Robert, count of Flanders, in the course of a pilgrimage to Jerusalem undertaken twelve years before the First Crusade, had stayed in the house of a certain elderly and learned Saracen, 'of very holy life, according to their standards'.[16] Albert of Aix, referring to the Egyptian occupation of Jerusalem in 1098-9, says that the 'King of Babylon' ruled justly and tolerantly and 'turned aside no Christian from the faith and order of his rule'.[17] Later, when describing the murder of Malducus (Mawdūd of Mosul) by the command of Dochinus (Tughtakīn of Damascus), he says that Dochinus earned much hatred among his own people, on account of the treachery implied by his instigation of this horrible deed, and the fact that it was done while Malducus was at prayer.[18] The Turks who oppose the author of the *Gesta* are never mean adversaries; they may howl and gabble and cry, but it is with fury and not with fear, and the 'devilish word which I do not understand', which they shouted as a war-cry at the battle of Dorylaeum,[19] is transliterated by Ralph of Caen as 'Allachibar', which must surely be *'Allāh akbar'*, 'God is Great'.[20]

According to the Frankish writers, the Muslims accepted a dual authority not unlike that symbolised by the Two Swords in the west. The author of the *Gesta* makes Kerbogha begin his imaginary bombastic despatch to Persia with the words 'To the Caliph our Pope *(nostro apostolico)* and the Lord Sultan our King ... greeting and boundless honour'.[21] Elsewhere he explains that Kerbogha had been given licence to kill Christians by the caliph 'who is the pope of the Turks'.[22] Guibert of Nogent amplifies this by saying that the Saracens call the kings of Persia 'sultans', as the Romans call theirs 'Caesars', and that the caliph is 'the chief pontiff of their error, for they have their own pope, just as our people do'.[23] All the Frankish chroniclers agree that the Muslims worship in mosques, which they call *bafumarie* or *machumarie* (the origin of our word 'mummery'). The *Gesta* describes the burial of the dead Turks at Antioch in stone tombs around the mosque, with an abundant supply of precious grave-goods, including clothes, money and weapons. This burial of grave-goods is not a usual Muslim practice, but since the author of the *Gesta* was himself present at the destruction of these Muslim tombs, and had no reason for inventing the story, it seems likely that his testimony in this instance is accurate.[24] Albert of Aix, in describing the death of Mawdūd (who was murdered by the Assassins while attending a mosque), says that the *amīr*, a most religious man, was stabbed 'while he was in a secret part of his oratory on a festival day, and intent upon the ceremonies',[25] but the author of the *Gesta* disparagingly calls a mosque 'a devil's chapel'.[26] The Christians always assumed that these mosques contained idols, representing Mahomet or the multiplicity of gods on whom Muslims were assumed to call in times of trouble. It may be that some Franks heard their enemies calling, with perfect orthodoxy, upon Allāh by some of His ninety-nine 'most beautiful names', and assumed these to be the names of many different gods. The author of the *Gesta* represents Kerbogha as taking an oath 'by Mahomet and all the names of the gods',[27] and inquiring from his mother whether Bohemond and Tancred are not the gods of the Franks, who deliver them from their enemies.[28] Later, in the course of the battle of Ascalon, he makes al-Afḍal call upon 'Mahomet and all the gods' to witness that he will never raise another army.[29] Robert the Monk, embroidering upon the account given in the *Gesta*, attributes to al-Afḍal the complaint 'O Mahomet, Mahomet, who ever served you with fairer devotion than I did, with images of you most beautifully adorned, and all the proper rites and ceremonies?'[30] Fulcher mentions (though he did not claim to have seen) 'an image made in the name of Mahomet' standing in the church of the Holy Sepulchre itself.[31] The fact that no idols were found, or ever could have been found, in captured mosques did not in the least deter Christian writers from inventing them. Ralph of Caen, in the *Gesta Tancredi*, tells a very curious story of how Tancred, after the taking of Jerusalem, entered into the Temple and found there a lofty throne, upon which was set an image richly adorned with gems and gold. 'Whose is this image?' he inquired 'Can it be Mars or Apollo? It cannot be

Christ; there is no sign of Christ here, no cross, no nails, no wounded side. This is no Christ but the first Antichrist, the wicked, the pernicious Mahomet. Oh, if only I had his comrade here too, the Antichrist who is to come, how I could trample both of them under my feet!' Lacking the opportunity to show the second Antichrist exactly what he thought of him, Tancred relieved his feelings by dashing down the image, which was 'precious in material but vile in form', and breaking it in pieces,[32] which he doubtless appropriated. The story is an odd one. It is of course reported at second hand, and, if Ralph did not invent it, it must rest upon the testimony of Tancred himself or one of his companions, since there is no trace of it in the eyewitness accounts of the First Crusade. Tancred himself, brought up in southern Italy, probably spoke some Arabic and knew something of Muslims. It is difficult to make out what lies behind the tale, since there seems to have been no general tendency to equate Mahomet with Antichrist. Later western writers often represented him as a devil, but usually as a minor or even a rather comical one. He is represented in the York cycle as the god upon whom the raging Herod calls, and he sometimes appears, in the rather down-at-heel company of 'Ribald' and 'Termagant', as one of the auxiliary fiends called up by Satan to resist Christ at the time of the Harrowing of Hell.

In addition to their attendance at mosques (and the Frankish writers never accused them of any lack of devotion) the Muslims were supposed to be much given to the study of astrology and of the magical arts in general. That learned and virtuous Saracen, in whose house Robert of Flanders stayed, returned one day from the mosque, according to Guibert of Nogent, saddened because it had been revealed to him in the stars that the Christians should one day recapture Jerusalem.[33] Kerbogha's sinister mother, as depicted in the *Gesta Francorum*, had 'looked into the sky, and studied the planets and the twelve signs of the Zodiac and all kinds of omens'.[34] She seems to have been more accurate in her prognostications than was the sultan, for she foretold Kerbogha's coming defeat, while the sultan, who according to Albert of Aix had consulted 'wise men, diviners and soothsayers', obtained from them confident predictions of a Muslim victory.[35] Raymond of Agiles has an odd tale of two women who, during the siege of Jerusalem in 1099, tried to bewitch a Frankish catapult. They seem to have been poor hands at the game, since a stone from the same catapult killed them and three of their children, a fate which Raymond records with obvious satisfaction.[36]

In the first half of the twelfth century there are signs that the Franks of Outremer and the Muslims of the western provinces of the ʿAbbasid empire were being driven by political necessity into a fair state of mutual forbearance. It became possible for a king of Jerusalem to negotiate a treaty with the ruler of Damascus, and for the local Christians and Muslims to combine forces in an attempt to ward off the threat of conquest by the *amīr* of Mosul in the name of the sultan of Bagdad. On the other side Usāma, though he regarded the Franks as being in some ways fearful barbarians, and was horrified at the idea that his son might grow up among them, was quite attached to some of his individual Frankish friends. Some of the Templars, he says, knew in which direction Mecca lay, and were prepared to turn on a mannerless Frankish pilgrim, newly come from the west, who tried to interrupt a Muslim gentleman at his prayers. In fact, western pilgrims, who came out for a few weeks and failed to settle in, were clearly something of a thorn in the side of the permanent Frankish inhabitants of Outremer. They were full of ill-regulated enthusiasms and had no grasp of local diplomacy.

Religious toleration in our sense would have been alien to the people of the eleventh and twelfth centuries, who neither understood nor desired it. Both Christians and Muslims regarded themselves, without compromise, as guardians of a revelation of the whole truth, and to both of them Jerusalem was a holy city. There could be no lasting agreement to differ, and no permanent truce, between them; but there was always, I think, a certain amount of mutual respect.

ROSALIND HILL

1. *Gesta Francorum* (ed. R. Hill), London, 1962, 21.(hereafter *G. F.*)

2. ibid: 51.

3. ibid: 67.

4. ibid: 96. (I am indebted to Dr. Smail, Professor R. Allen Brown and Mr. P. Lewis for helpful suggestions on this point).

5. Migne, *Patrologia Latina*, vol.166, 1086.(hereafter *P. L.*)

6. *P. L.* vol.155, 925.

7. Steven Runciman, *A History of the Crusades*, III, Cambridge, 1954, 59.

8. *The Oxford Book of Ballads* (ed. A. Quiller-Couch), Oxford, 1910, 199-205.

9. *G. F.*, 46, 96.

10. H.A.R. Gibb (ed. and tr.), *The Damascus Chronicle of the Crusades*, London, 1932, 66.

11. *P. L.*, vol.156, 689.

12. ibid: 691-2.

13. ibid: 685, *P. L.*, vol.155, 609 (Raymond of Agiles). ibid: 828 (Fulcher of Chartres). *G. F.*, 83.

14. *G. F.*, 49.

15. *P. L.*, vol.155, 828.

16. *P. L.*, vol.156, 816.

17. *P. L.*, vol.166 553.

18. *P. L.*, vol.166, 705-6. Compare *Damascus Chronicle*, 140.

19. *G. F.*, 18.

20. *P. L.*, vol.155, 521.

21. *G. F.*, 52.

22. ibid: 49.

23. *P. L.*, vol.156, 754.

24. *G. F.*, 42.

25. *P. L.*, vol.166, 706.

26. *G. F.*, 42.

27. ibid: 52.

28. ibid: 55-6.

29. ibid: 96.

30. *P. L.*, vol.155, 755.

31. ibid: 852.

32. ibid: 571.

33. *P. L.*, vol.156, 816.

34. *G. F.*, 55.

35. *P. L.*, vol.166, 483.

36. *P. L.*, vol.155, 658.

The survival in Latin Palestine of Muslim administration

In this paper I want to draw together various pieces of research undertaken by me in the past few years.[1] I will suggest that the general belief that the instruments of government in the Latin kingdom of Jerusalem were primitive is mistaken, for in fact many of them were comparatively sophisticated and well-developed, being inherited from the earlier Muslim rule. And I will try to put forward on that basis some of the lines one could take on the history of the kingdom.

Although, owing to the work of Professors Jean Richard and Joshua Prawer,[2] no-one would now consider the kingdom of Jerusalem to have been an ossified feudal state, incapable of development or growth, there is still a tendency to view its institutions of government as being of the simplest type, reflecting the decentralisation in Palestine in their primitive forms. On the face of it there are grounds for doubting this orthodoxy. The Latins in Palestine were a minority governing an indigenous majority; they were dependent on a far wider market than that encompassed by the frontiers of the kingdom; and they controlled and exploited the termini of one of the great trade-routes to the East. Were they unlike any invaders before or since in that they did not make use of the governmental machinery they found on their arrival, a machinery which, in spite of the disorders in the Near East in the half-century before the First Crusade, must still have had some existence? An answer to this question can only be found by examining historical material which is far from satisfactory, searching for officials and offices the titles of which were transliterations from or translations of Arabic; or for clues to the existence of bureaux which, although called by different names, were working in the same way as counterparts in the Muslim world. The first historian to approach the question in this way was Professor Claude Cahen, especially with regard to the principality of Antioch which will not be treated by me here, and Professor Joshua Prawer has also made a significant contribution.[3] I have tried merely to push a little further along the same road, but it is a dangerous one to follow, because it is sometimes all too easy to think that one has found what one is looking for when in fact one has simply read too much into the evidence. Other factors greatly complicate the task. The evidence is distorted by the chance survival in fair numbers of certain kinds of document and the loss of most of the rest. We have one more or less complete collection of deeds concerning a lay fief, which survived because at an early stage it was incorporated into the archives of the Teutonic Knights, one incomplete list, dating from the 1180s, of fief-holders and their services, and one list of the entry and sales duties to be charged in Acre in the mid-thirteenth century, but in the main the charters, letters and inventories at our disposal are those of the religious orders and the communities of European merchants, who had houses or centres in the West to which their archives could be sent for safe-keeping. Our knowledge is therefore one-sided and we often have to approach subjects indirectly, getting, for instance, some idea of the way customs houses and markets functioned from studies of exemptions from their workings granted to merchants. And the scarcity of the documents often means arriving at conclusions on a comparison of phrases in charters separated by a long way in space and time. This is especially perilous because in the area there were regional variations: the markets in Antioch, Tyre and Acre were run in different ways; and weights and measures seem to have differed in districts as close to one another as Ramla and Ascalon. The westerners, moreover, arrived in the East with attitudes which they found impossible to eradicate. One finds the creation of feudal sergeantries to provide minor offices in a country with a monetary economy where salaries could easily have been paid, although there were already in the East institutions such as the *iqṭāʿ* and the *ḍamān* which the Franks would have found easy to feudalise. And the Franks, coming from an area in which jurisdiction was usually linked to the raising of revenues, found it hard to cope with a machinery of government in which finance and jurisdiction functioned separately: in Palestine they seem to have incorporated many of the financial offices into the hierarchy of their courts, either by turning local *sekretas* or *dīwāns* into tribunals or by attaching them to one of their own courts. Again, in the Christian West there was a much clearer distinction made between temporal and spiritual jurisdictions than in Islam or Judaism. The Franks created special lay courts for the indigenous population, probably allowing the non-Christians to answer to their *qāḍīs* and rabbis on what they, the Franks, considered to be religious questions, and presumably often introducing a differentiation in legal cases that must have been alien and incomprehensible to the Muslims and Jews.

A glance at the Palestinian countryside under Latin rule reveals a scene which is consistent with the history of the area, apart from occasional colonial settlements organised on western lines[4] and odd patches of demesne land, especially gardens and sugar-cane plantations down near the coast.[5] A village, under a headman similar to the modern *mukhtār*[6] but known to the Latins as a *rays (ra'īs)*, acted as a community, making common decisions on the cultivation of arable lands. Since there was very little demesne the villagers were subject to minimal labour services. The arable lands were divided among them and they also possessed gardens, olive groves and vineyards similar to the modern *ḥawākīr* lands. Many villages had *khirbas* attached to them. The villagers paid their lords *kharāj* and other dues, among them one very similar to the Egyptian *marā'ī*, and a forced gift which, at least in the principality of Antioch, was given a name that appears to be a transliteration of the Arabic *mu'na*. As in Egypt, there was a tendency for these charges in kind to be commuted for money payments. There seems to be no real evidence for the practice of *mushā'*, which is so common today,[7] but one can conclude that we have as it were a curtain suddenly drawn back, revealing a system of agriculture subject of course to change and development, but entirely consistent with the traditions of the area and the farming practices which survive today.

Turning from the villages themselves to the links between them and their usually absentee landlords, who would have had little reason to visit their estates except at harvest time when the crops were apportioned, it is not surprising to find that the origins of the two officials who represented the lord probably lay in Muslim government. The first of these was an officer usually called a dragoman. His title was a corrupt transliteration of the Arabic *turjumān*, meaning interpreter, and indeed he is sometimes to be found in the documents with the Latin title of *interpres*. The powers and status of the dragomans known to us varied. Some exercised authority throughout, and some only in a subdivision of, a lordship; some were responsible for the scattered estates of a church and some acted on behalf of the minor fiefs in the royal domain near Acre, where the right to have one's own dragoman seems to have been granted as a special privilege to the tenants. Some dragomans were knights, some lay burgesses, some sergeants, but on lay fiefs the dragomanate had usually been feudalised, becoming a sergeantry for the maintenance of which the holder received a proportion of the crops of the villages he supervised. Although we know that dragomans rode through the villages in their charge, presumably inspecting them on their lords' behalf, there is very little evidence on their duties. We find them acting as interpreters, as we would expect, and as intermediaries between lords and village headmen. We must assume that they were bailiffs or overseers of some kind, perhaps with powers of supervision of jurisdiction, since revenues were dealt with by the *scribae*, the lords' other intermediaries. And it should be remembered that lords would originally have needed interpreters and that such an official already existed in the Muslim world, the *mutarjim*, an assistant to the *qāḍī* in his dealings with the many people under Muslim rule. This office, or one like it, may have been the basis of the dragomanate, being taken over by the lords who were in some ways heirs to the jurisdiction of the *qāḍīs*.

The other official was known as the *scriba*, a title of course given to many different sorts of person, including those who merely wrote out charters. But it is quite easy to pick out our *scribae* from the rest. We can identify them in quite a large number of lordships and a very high proportion of them were indigenous: 14, perhaps 16, out of 25. Some, especially the Latins among them, were quite considerable persons, the holders of sergeantries and members of local Burgess Courts. One of the native-born was himself the son of an official. Among them were a group called *scribani*, who may be differentiated from the rest because they held their offices in fief as sergeantries: here perhaps the Latins had taken over and feudalised the Muslim *ḍamān* or tax farm. Like the dragomans the holders of these sergeantries, one of whom was a knight, enjoyed rents in kind. Six examples of the *scribanage* survive. Two of them suggest that the tenants of small fiefs near Acre were given the right to have their own *scribae* as well as dragomans; but a contrasting case in southern Palestine suggests that a lord's *scribanus* could have authority even over villages in rear-fiefs if the tenants had not been given the right to possess their own *scribae*. The *scriba* was responsible for the collection of revenues, assembled the people of a district when boundary disputes were being decided and was assumed to have knowledge of the names and holdings of the peasants in his area. He was clearly a financial official and collector of taxes, perhaps combining the duties of the various Fatimid officials who collected the *kharāj* and the *jizya* tax on non-Muslims. It is clear that the title of *scriba* was merely a translation of the Arabic *kātib*, used of officials in Muslim cadastral offices.[8]

So far we have seen that most villages in Frankish Palestine functioned in a traditional way and that in the officials linking them to their new Christian lords there was continuity from the Muslim past. One finds the same sort of situation in the towns, although the clear distinction between jurisdiction and finance, which existed under Muslim rule, was broken up as the Franks turned the financial offices, except the *amwāl* and in most towns the gates, into courts. In general terms the judicial system may be summarised as follows: the crown in the royal domain and the lords in their seigneuries inherited the powers of ordinary, and extraordinary, jurisdiction and cases relating to their vassals were decided in their seigneurial courts; *shurṭa*, criminal jurisdiction, in so far as it applied to ordinary freemen, was imposed on the lord's behalf by the viscount, who presided over the Burgess Court in each Latin settlement, assisted by officials called *placiers*, who may have been responsible for town quarters; *ḥisba*, commercial jurisdiction, was, except perhaps in Tyre, imposed by each Burgess Court and also by a subordinate market court, the *Cour de la Fonde*, while in a port the customs house was converted into another court subordinate to the Burgess Court, the *Cour de la Mer* or *de la Chaine*; there was created the *Cour des Syriens*, a special court, also subordinate to the Burgess Court, to cope with 'secular' cases concerning non-Latins, while 'spiritual' cases were allowed to go as before to the Eastern bishops and the rabbis and presumably also the *qāḍīs*.[9]

These courts collected revenues as well as making judgements. I will deal with the ports, gates and markets later, but the Burgess

Court and perhaps the *Cour des Syriens* were responsible for collecting various dues. They gathered rents on houses, a charge on burgess properties known as *tallea* which was some sort of seigneurial due, and a capitation tax which in Tyre was imposed on Jews at the rate of 1 besant a year but was also, it seems, levied on Muslims and appears to be the old *jizya* tax on *dhimmīs*, now lifted from Christians of all denominations but maintained on Jews and imposed on Muslims. Retail shopkeepers, stall-holders and artisans were probably subject to a charge called *mensuragium* on weights and measures and what appears to have been Muslim *hilālī* taxes, licence fees paid monthly to the government: in Tyre Syrian dye-workers paid 2 caroubles a month for each of their vats and the Muslim origins of the tax are also suggested by the fact that in Tyre it was collected by a *muḥtasib*. Probably also subject to *hilālī*, as in Muslim countries, were the owners of public baths and ovens and money-changers, whose tables certainly provided revenue for their lords. Finally there was a curious tax, to be found only in Tyre, paid by pork butchers at the rate of 4 *denarii* for every pig slaughtered. Its name, *tuazo*, may be linked to *tawaḍḍu'*, an Arabic word for ritual ablutions and this, together with the absurdity of a Christian government imposing taxes on meat which was not unclean to it, would suggest that *tuazo* was a survival from Fatimid times maintained by the Franks.[10]

If one compares the working of ports and markets like those of Acre with Muslim Alexandria or Byzantine Constantinople the parallels are so striking as to leave one in no doubt that, whatever the changes in details, the Christian commercial centres continued to be operated as they always had been. In Acre the arrival of a ship was signalled by the tolling of a bell and it was met by what seems to have been a pilot boat which probably escorted it to a berth out in the centre of the harbour. As in Egypt the cargo must then have been ferried to the land, while a port tax, known as *anchoragia*, was levied on the ship, although, unlike Egypt, this does not seem to have varied according to the vessel's size. An additional tax, the *terciaria*, was estimated on the numbers of passengers and crew. As in Egypt and the Byzantine empire the goods taken to the shore were inspected by customs officials and registered for taxation on an *ad valorem* basis, although there were always commodities like wine, oil and grain on which the duty was charged on quantity rather than on value. As in Byzantium nothing was levied at this stage on goods destined for sale in the markets, as opposed to those brought in for personal consumption or re-export, for a combined entry and sales charge was taken in the markets on most goods, although it must be admitted that here the evidence is rather ambiguous and it is possible that some goods were sold on the quayside under the supervision of the customs officials. Most, however, went to the markets, being subject there to a total *ad valorem* charge which varied according to the commodity but was generally lower than the Egyptian *khums* of 20% and often higher than the Byzantine *kommerkion* of 10%: in the middle of the thirteenth century 11 5/24% seems to have been regarded as standard. As in Egypt these dues were probably levied in two different ways, according to the method of sale prevalent in the markets. There must have been man-to-man bargains between merchants and here probably there were official price-lists which established the theoretical value of the goods exchanged; and, since we know of auctioneers, there were possibly public auctions like the Egyptian *ḥalqas*; at them the duty must have been sliced off the proceeds by the auctioneers. It is clear that, as in Egypt and Byzantium, the charges were shared by seller and buyer. Dues on exports were levied on the quayside, as in Egypt, being imposed even on re-exports which had not been sold in the markets, and the customs house had its own weights and measures, although it is not as clear that there was a consistent method of establishing what was due - some goods seem to have been charged *ad valorem* and some according to quantity. But, as in Egypt, it seems that a charge was made on the difference in value between a merchant's imports and exports if the latter was higher than the former.

Close inspection reveals that a port like Acre worked very much in accord with East Mediterranean practice. Three bureaux, two of which were also courts, oversaw commerce. First there was on the portside the *Chaine* or *Cathena*, which took its name from the chain stretched across the harbour entrance. The office, in Acre a *khān*-like building on the port side, was, at least from the mid-twelfth century, a maritime court concerning itself with the law of the sea and maritime contracts, although any matter involving more than 1 silver mark went to the Burgess Court, in which case the *bailli* and jurors of the *Cour de la Chaine* conducted a preliminary enquiry. It was also the body responsible for the running and upkeep of the port; a department accounting revenues and paying out rents; and a customs house, staffed by *baillis* or *custodes* and employing *scribae*.

Secondly the gates of the towns, and certainly those of Jerusalem, Tyre, Beirut, Tripoli and Ascalon, were usually administered by their own offices. The gate officials, like those on the quayside, laid a charge on imports and exports, though, as in the port, imports for sale in the markets were probably not taxed until the sale had taken place. The gate officials could demand from a man an oath that he was bringing in a commodity for his own use, in which case he merely paid a passage tax. There is a puzzling absence of references in the documents to the revenues from the gates of Acre, although officials certainly levied dues at them. It may have been that the gates of Acre came under the *Cour de la Fonde*, the market court which in that city also carried out the functions of a local *Cour des Syriens*, but the Muslim traveller Ibn Jubayr reported of his arrival in Acre in 1184 that the Christian scribes, who in a *khān* inspected and registered baggage and made out their accounts in Arabic, were employed in a *dīwān* held in farm by a man honoured with the title of *ṣāḥib*.[11] It is therefore probable that the silence of the documents on the revenues from the gates of Acre was because they were held in farm.

Thirdly there were the markets, the goal of any merchant who had entered the town through the port or the land gates. In Acre and in some other towns the more important markets seem to have been run by officials of the *fonde* or *funda*. These words, and the related *fonticum/fondicum*, were corruptions of the Arabic *funduq*, itself a transliteration of the Greek *pandokeia*, and were to be found in many countries bordering on the Mediterranean. In Latin Syria the word *fonde* could mean first a *khān*-like building; secondly a market in a *khān*-like building which could belong to an individual owner or, as in Egypt, could be devoted to the sale of a particular commodity; thirdly, not one but a group of markets under a single administration - in Acre, for instance, the royal *fonde* was a group of open squares and markets in the vicinity of the *funda regis*, presumably the building from which they were run, while the word *fonde* seems also to have been applied to the Italian markets down near the harbour; and fourthly not the markets themselves but their administration, the *bailli* and jurors of the *Cour de la Fonde* who concerned themselves with minor court cases on commerce, debts and the like. In Acre the *Cour de la Fonde* also acted as a court of the first instance for the indigenous population, and in most towns it controlled the office staffed by sergeants, auctioneers, *scribae (kātibs)* and measurers which oversaw the work of the *coretiers* who ran the individual markets, levied tolls, accounted revenues and paid out money-fiefs and rents. It must be stressed that in the cities there were always some markets administered separately from the *fondes* and that it is possible that in Tyre, the second city of the kingdom, all markets were semi-independent: there the markets may have been under the general supervision of a *muḥtasib* - it is noteworthy that the only reference to this official in Latin Palestine is to be found with regard to Tyre between 1210 and 1243 and that he was functioning there very much like the judge he was in Muslim centres.

The various offices in the cities seem to have been quite sophisticated. They not only collected tolls and market charges, probably rendering accounts to the *secrete*, but also paid out money-fiefs and rents granted on the proceeds from commerce by the kings and great lords to vassals and churches. These payments of money-fiefs and rents were made at fixed times in the year, most commonly quarterly; we know that in Tyre the financial year began on 1 November. It was even possible for a man who held a money-fief to create out of it a rear-fief or make an eleemosynary grant to a religious order, the resulting payment being made not by him but by the office involved. This suggests fairly good bureaucratic procedures, presumably inherited from the Muslim *dīwāns* out of which the offices must have grown.[12]

So far we have seen that a lord's means of exploiting the countryside and towns were very similar to those of the Muslim rulers before him. Since we have come across references to *scribae* or *kātibs* in ports and markets as well as villages it is worth asking whether the cadastral offices had survived. We know quite a lot about the *Grant Secrete*, the chief financial office in the kingdom. Supervised by the seneschal, one of the great officers of the crown, it employed its own scribes, differentiated from those 'in the royal household', presumably the *camera*. In it were registered the boundaries of fiefs and the services owed for them and also lists of *fief-rentes*. It paid *restor* for the replacement of horses lost or injured in the performance of military service. To it accounts were made of the revenues collected by royal agents and courts. It contained records of the standard measurement of the Frankish carrucate and perhaps also of the royal *modius*. As its name implies, it was clearly a financial office and department of registration on the lines of a Greek *sekreta* or Muslim *dīwān*, having duties similar to the Fatimid *bayt (dīwān) al-māl* - and indeed it was called the *amwāl* by two Muslim contemporary writers - together with the functions of several subordinate Muslim offices which oversaw *iqṭā'*s and collected the poll-tax from *dhimmīs*, estate duties and village revenues.

There survive no direct references to *secretes* in Palestine outside the royal domain, although the principality of Antioch had its own *secrete* with registers dating from before the Latins' arrival. But we know from a document of 1243 that besides the *Grant Secrete* in Acre there was another *secrete* in Tyre, also part of the royal domain. This would suggest that *secretes* could be attached to localities and the existence of *scribae* in the lordships of Arsur, Jaffa/Ascalon, Beaufort, Beirut, Caesarea, Chastiau-dou-rei, Galilee, the fief of Geoffrey Le Tor, Gibelet in the county of Tripoli, Haifa, Margat in the principality of Antioch, Nābulus, Nazareth, Ramla, Scandelion and Tyre leads one to assume that the lordships as well as the royal domain had inherited cadastral offices from the Muslim past.[13] Continuity is made even more likely by the significant number of examples of the boundaries of fiefs following those of earlier units of administration: for instance that part of the principality of Galilee which was in Palestine proper had boundaries nearly co-terminous with Byzantine Palaestina Secunda; the lordship of Caesarea had the same borders as had the city territory of Caesarea in the seventh century; the lordship of Arsur covered the same area as had the Muslim *kūra* of Arsūf.[14]

So far I have tried to demonstrate the very real way in which the Muslim administrative system survived under the Franks, providing them with the means of exploiting their seigneurial rights in the villages and towns and drawing off revenues from the ports and markets that lay at the end of the trade route to the East. And the picture I have tried to draw leads to several conclusions. It cannot be denied that the instruments of government were fairly sophisticated. It is the decentralised state of the kingdom that has confused historians who are used to seeing the development of the organs of government in Europe following centralisation. In Latin Jerusalem the lords in their great fiefs were in many ways nearly independent of the crown, having full rights of justice and at least from the later twelfth century the right to make peace or war with the Muslims without reference to the kings or regents. But in Jerusalem a fragmented authority did not mean an underdeveloped administration precisely because the crown in the royal domain and the lords in their lordships had all inherited centres of developed administration: the kingdom was, in other words, scattered with little nuclei of advanced government. An understanding of the easternness of the administration, moreover, and how it worked, helps one to explain oddities. Elsewhere I have shown how the absence of demesne lands affected the tithes-privileges of the exempt Orders of the Church,[15] and how it was in fact in the interest of the kings and lords to grant what seem on the surface to be vast commercial rights to European merchants: my conclusion was that on balance the granters gained, especially as loopholes were systematically covered and a very close watch was kept on the kinds of privilege granted.[16]

Having at their disposal a fairly advanced bureaucracy, the kings and nobles of Jerusalem were, at least for a time, *potentially* rich. Matthew Paris, the great English chronicler, had heard from Richard of Cornwall, who was in the East in 1240-41, that he had been told by the brothers of the Temple and the Hospital that the city of Acre was worth to its lord £50,000 *per annum* - and Matthew seems to have been referring to pounds sterling. The sum may well be exaggerated and is given at third hand, but it is startling to find a contemporary maintaining that Acre alone provided more than the normal annual revenues of the crown of England.[17] This reputation for wealth may go some way towards explaining the interest in Palestine of western rulers like Frederick II or Charles of Anjou, and the wealth of the crown, at any rate before the decline of Acre and Tyre from about 1250 onwards, would enable it to have had a certain independence of the feudatories: the constitutional opposition to the kings, revealing a fear of arbitrary actions, is incomprehensible if the crown was always weak.[18]

In the light of the crown's potential wealth and the income it gained from the ports, some reassessment ought to be made of the kingdom's military strength in the thirteenth century. Before 1187 the king could call on the service of c.700 knights. The great territorial losses following the annihilation of the Christian army at Ḥaṭṭīn, most of which were never recovered, should have meant a drastic fall in the number of fiefs. But it seems that the Latin army which fought the battle of Gaza in 1244, although smaller and bolstered by contingents from Cyprus and Antioch-Tripoli, was not nearly so small as one would suppose, given the territorial losses that had been incurred. It seems likely that these losses in land had been offset to some extent by the increase in revenues from the ports which could be granted out in money-fiefs. Some of these money-fiefs were large enough for rear-fiefs to be created out of them: for instance in 1229 Frederick II gave Conrad of Hohenlohe 6,000 besants a year from the port or market revenues of Acre in return for personal service together with 9 knights. There is, moreover, evidence to suggest that in the first half of the thirteenth century Acre was an important centre for mercenaries. Of course the Church, the Military Orders and the great feudatories were all employers of fighting men, but so too was the central government. With a less reduced feudal host than has been assumed and a larger professional wing, supplemented by the certain growth in the commitment of the Military Orders, it would be rash to suppose that at least before 1250 the military forces at the disposal of the kingdom were markedly inferior to those of the twelfth century.[19]

The great feudatories also benefitted from the commercial prosperity of the Latin East, often, it must be admitted, at the crown's expense. One finds them at the end of the twelfth century usurping the regalian right to mint coins, which incidentally is evidence for the need for money in their fiefs; by the mid-thirteent century gaining control over public roads which had possibly been subject to regalian right; and building up the ports in their fiefs. A twelfth-century law had reserved the possession of ports dealing in international trade to the monarch, making it an offence for a lord to:

> build a port in his land for ships and vessels and a road into paynim, to improve his land and diminish the rights of the crown.

But Tyre, which until the 1240s was part of the royal domain, retained its commercial importance under the de Montfort lords. Jaffa for much of the period an apanage of the crown, was from the first a major point of disembarkation for pilgrims and from the 1120s was involved in commerce. A century later sea-trade linked it to Antioc and in the 1250s, under the great Count John, it was growing in importance: in 1253 the pope offered an indulgence to all who helpe John rebuild it and in the 1260s, indeed, it seems to have been used as a supply port for the Egyptian army, although it was still in Christian hands. In the 1160s Haifa and Caesarea were involved at least in local coastal traffic and in 1234 the lord of Haifa grantec privileges to the Genoese. Between 1221 and 1223 the lord of Beirut gave commercial rights to merchants from Genoa, Venice and Marseille His markets were already dealing not only in local products - potter wine, oil, corn, sugar, dyes, glass and soap - but also in commoditi from further afield - silk, bombazine, wool and cloth, flax and line brazil-wood, pepper, incense, spices, indigo, pearls and precious stones. By the second half of the thirteenth century Beirut already had a flourishing Genoese colony and was on the way to becoming an important Levantine port.[20]

Although there survives only one direct reference to the wealth of one of these lords,[21] we may assume that at least as long as the trade routes ran in their favour they had large incomes. This can also be deduced from the fact that it was they who shouldered the chief burdens of the defence of Palestine. In 1261 the Master of the Templars, writing of his own Order's commitment, claimed that:

> there is not a prince of this world who on one and the same day could hold seven great castles without much inconvenience and keep them in a defensible state against this multitude [the Mongols].

The surviving evidence for the expenses of garrisoning, supplying and maintaining castles in the East bears the Master out. But at the time he was writing it was not his Order, nor that of the Hospital, nor the crown which held most of the great castles in

Palestine. Beirut, Tyre, Toron, Haifa, Caesarea, Arsur (Arsūf) and Jaffa were in the hands of lay lords. It is true that Sidon and Beaufort had just been renounced and leased to the Templars and that Arsur was soon to be leased to the Hospitallers. But Caesarea and Jaffa were in lay hands when they fell to the Egyptians in 1265 and 1268 and so until the end in 1291 remained Haifa, Scandelion, Tyre and Beirut.[22] It must be stressed that the feudatories did not have the international assets of the great Orders and must, therefore, have had large incomes, even though their expenses would have been high. Their wealth makes the extraordinary rise among the feudal class of an important group of learned and articulate jurists more comprehensible. Of course there were other reasons for this, particularly the legal practices of the kingdom and the history of jurisprudence there, but the existence of a town-dwelling class of knights, rich enough to spare the time to devote to the study of the law, is surely significant.[23]

The crown and lords of Jerusalem were potentially rich, but their wealth was precariously based and the great burdens that defence imposed on them meant that any change in the equilibrium of economic activity would affect their ability to survive. No doubt the responsibilities of defence were bearable before the 1240s, when the trade routes were running in their favour and relations with Islam were comparatively peaceful - this period coincided with the lords' greatest political activity - but after 1250, with the coming to power of the Mamluks, the arrival of the Mongols and the decline of the Levantine ports, the burdens must have become nearly insupportable. Unlike their western cousins the Palestinian lords could not retrench when in difficulties, for their ability to resist the enemy would be affected. It is, therefore, not surprising that the constitutional history of the kingdom of Jerusalem is particularly affected by its institutional history. Both crown and baronage were very sensitive to threats to their incomes, which came partly from lands, but above all from town revenues.

It should be clear that the wealth of the kingdom of Jerusalem was very dependent on the commercial traffic passing above all from the great entrepôt of Damascus down to the Palestinian coast, which, incidentally, explains the strength of those parties in the kingdom which favoured treaties with Damascus. It does seem that this traffic perceptibly increased from 1180, before which the Red Sea route from the East to Alexandria and Damietta had been dominant, until about 1260, when the conflicts between Mamluks and Mongols disturbed the Syrian hinterland and a major route from the East developed north of the Levant in the areas under Mongol control, with as termini Ayas on the Gulf of Alexandretta and the Black Sea ports. For a period of about eighty years the cities of Acre, Tyre and Tripoli were among the most important in the east Mediterranean and were centres of the economic life of the whole region, whether in Muslim or Christian hands. It has been suggested that the pacific policy towards the Franks of the Ayyubids was conditioned partly by the economic importance of the Christians to them[24] and there is evidence that even Baybars was conscious that the economy of his Syrian possessions depended on Acre.[25] But by Baybars' time the situation was changing: commercial traffic was declining and Christian Palestine was coming to be dependent for its survival on the West. In this respect the crucial date in the kingdom's history was not 1187 but 1250-60 when the pattern of trade began to change and the Mamluks and Mongols arrived on the scene. At any rate the first half of the thirteenth century, although it had its times of peril, was far more prosperous than is usually assumed and the Franks had far more sophisticated instruments for taking advantage of that prosperity than is often realised.

JONATHAN RILEY-SMITH

1. 'Some lesser officials in Latin Syria', *English Historical Review* LXXXVII, 1972; 'Government in Latin Syria and the Commercial Privileges of Foreign Merchants', *Relations between East and West in the Middle Ages*, ed. D. Baker, Edinburgh, 1973; *The Feudal Nobility and the Kingdom of Jerusalem*, London, 1973 40-98 *passim*.

2. J. Richard, *Le royaume latin de Jérusalem*, Paris, 1953; J. Prawer, 'Les premiers temps de la féodalité du royaume de Jérusalem', *Tijdschrift voor rechtsgeschiedenis*, XXII, 1954; J. Prawer, 'La noblesse et le régime féodal du royaume latin de Jérusalem', *Le Moyen âge* , LXV, 1959: J. Prawer, 'Etude sur le droit des Assises de Jérusalem', *Revue historique de droit français et étranger*, sér.4, XXXIX-XL, 1961-2; J. Prawer, *Histoire du royaume latin de Jérusalem*, Paris, 1969-70: J. Prawer, *The Latin Kingdom of Jerusalem*. London, 1972.

3. Cl. Cahen, *La Syrie du Nord a l'époque des croisades et la principaute franque d'Antioche*, Paris, 1940; Cl. Cahen, 'Notes sur l'histoire des croisades et de l'Orient latin. 2. Le régime rural syrien au temps de la domination franque. 3. Orient latin et commerce du Levant', *Bulletin de la Faculté des Lettres de l'Université de Strasbourg*, XXIX, 1950-51; Cl. Cahen,'La féodalité et les institutions politiques de l'Orient latin', *Oriente e Occidente nel Medioevo*, Academia nazionale dei Lincei. Fondazione 'Allessandro Volta'. XII Convegno 'Volta'. Rome, 1957; Cl. Cahen,'A propos des coutumes du marché d'Acre', *Revue historique de droit français et étranger*, Sér.4, XLI; 1963, J. Prawer, 'L'etablissement des coutumes du marché à Saint-Jean d'Acre et la date de composition du Livre des Assises des Bourgeois', *Revue historique de droit français et étranger*, Sér.4, XXIX, 1951; J. Prawer, 'Etude de quelques problèmes agraires et sociaux d'une seigneurie croisée au XIIIe siècle', *Byzantion* XXII-XXIII, 1952-3. See also E. G. Rey, *Les colonies franques de Syrie aux XIIème et XIIIème*

siècles, Paris, 1883; J. Richard, 'Colonies marchandes privilégiées et marché seigneurial. La Fonde d'Acre et ses "droitures"', *Le Moyen âge* LIX, 1953.

4. J. Prawer, 'Colonial Activities in the Latin Kingdom of Jerusalem', *Revue belge de philologie et d'histoire*, XXIX, 1951; Riley-Smith, *Feudal Nobility*, 49; M. Benvenisti, *The Crusaders in the Holy Land*, Jerusalem, 1970, 218-27.

5. Riley-Smith, op.cit., 46, 49-50.

6. There is in fact one reference to a *mukhtār*. *Urkunden zur älteren Handels- und Staatsgeschichte der Republik Venedig*, ed. G.L.F. Tafel and G. M. Thomas, Vienna, 1856-7, III, 400.

7. Riley-Smith, *Feudal Nobility*, 40-53; Riley-Smith, 'Some lesser officials', 9-15, Prawer, 'Etude de quelques problèmes agraires', *passim*; Cahen, 'Le régime rural', *passim*; Cahen, 'La féodalité', 184, 187-8.

8. Riley-Smith, 'Some lesser officials', 15-26; Riley-Smith, *Feudal Nobility*, 53-8.

9. Riley-Smith, *Feudal Nobility*, 85-98 *passim*; Riley-Smith, 'Some lesser officials', 2-9.

10. Riley-Smith, *Feudal Nobility*, 84.

11. Ibn Jobair, (Ibn Jubayr) *Voyages* (tr. Maurice Gaudefroy-Demombynes), III, Paris, 1953, 354.

12. Riley-Smith, 'Government and Commercial Privileges', *passim*; Riley-Smith, *Feudal Nobility*, 81-97.

13. Riley-Smith, 'Some lesser officials', 19-23; Riley-Smith, *Feudal Nobility*, 56-60.

14. M. Benvenisti, *The Crusaders*, 14, 132.

15. J.S.C. Riley-Smith, *The Knights of St. John in Jerusalem and Cyprus c. 1050-1310*, London, 1967, 391 ff.

16. Riley-Smith, 'Government and Commercial Privileges' *passim*; Riley-Smith, *Feudal Nobility*, 67-78.

17. Matthew Paris, 'Itinéraire de Londres à Jérusalem, (ed. H. Michelant and G. Raynaud), *Itinéraires à Jérusalem et descriptions de la Terre Sainte rédigés en français aux XIe, XIIe et XIIIe siècles*, Geneva, 1882, 137.

18. See Riley-Smith, *Feudal Nobility, passim*.

19. J.S.C. Riley-Smith, 'Historical Introduction' to U. and M.C. Lyons, *Ayyubids, Mamlukes and Crusaders*, Cambridge, 1971, II, xv-xviii; Riley-Smith, *Feudal Nobility*, 5-7. For Conrad of Hohenloe's fief, see 'Quatre pièces relatives à l'ordre teutonique en Orient', *Archives de l'Orient latin*, II, 166-7.

20. Riley-Smith, *Feudal Nobility*, 64-78.

21. John, the 'Old Lord' of Beirut. 'Les Gestes des Chiprois'; *Recueil des historiens des croisades. Documents arméniens*, II, 725.

22. Riley-Smith, *Feudal Nobility*, 28-32.

23. Riley-Smith, *Feudal Nobility*, *passim*.

24. H.A.R. Gibb 'The Aiyūbids', *A History of the Crusades*, (ed.-in-chief K. M. Setton) II, 2nd. edn., Madison, 1969. 694.

25. Lyons, *Ayyubids*, II, 43-4.

The international status of the Latin kingdom of Jerusalem, 1150-1192

I

A paper read to the Royal Historical Society some years ago considered a number of occasions in the period between the Second Crusade and the Third on which rulers of crusader states not only invited kings from western Europe to bring them help in defending Latin Syria, but also offered to serve within their own borders under the leadership of the royal visitors.[1] More recently Professor Hans Mayer has traversed some of the same ground, and has also extended the discussion by examining more fully attempts by rulers of the Latin East, and particularly by those of the kingdom of Jerusalem, to involve monarchs of the Christian West in the government and defence of the Holy Land, as well as a number of episodes in which Western kings intruded themselves into the affairs of Jerusalem on their own initiative and without invitation. He has also suggested a possible legal basis for such initiatives.[2]

The subject matter of these two papers was drawn mainly from the later twelfth century and it seems to show that during this period the international status of the crusader kingdom was unique. Professor Mayer has invited further discussion of the topic.[3] In this paper the peculiarities of the kingdom's international status will be described (sections II-VII). Sections VIII-XII are intended as a contribution to the discussion of the problems of explaining them.

II

Crusader Jerusalem was set apart from other contemporary Christian kingdoms by its *raison d'être*. Within its borders was the greatest of Christian shrines - the Holy Places. Those few square yards of ground, revered, certainly from the third century and almost certainly earlier, as the scene of Christ's crucifixion, burial and resurrection, were, and are, accommodated within a single building, the Church of the Holy Sepulchre. This church alone, to say nothing of a multitude of other biblical sites, attracted then, as it does now, a large annual influx of pilgrims.

They were sufficiently numerous and regular to make a valued contribution to the finances of royal government and sometimes to its military resources as well; they ultimately affected the development and perhaps the design of Italian shipping. They came from all parts of Western Christendom. They arrived in the spring, for the Easter festival, and generally went home at the end of the summer. The weeks they spent in that small country enabled them to become acquainted with its conditions and circumstances, which they duly recounted as they made their way home and after they had reached it. Pope Alexander III in an encyclical letter on the affairs of the Holy Land once referred to the *communis transeuntium relatio*, the common reports of travellers passing through Rome, who were among the sources of his information.[4]

The dissemination of news in that way left its mark on much of the history written in the twelfth and thirteenth centuries. The region of which some historians then knew most, other than their own, was the Holy Land, and this was likely to be true of many others besides. 'Every man' it used to be said 'has two countries, his own and France'. In the twelfth and thirteenth centuries there was a sense in which many had two countries, their own and the Latin kingdom of Jerusalem.

There was another recurrent phenomenon in that age which made the Latin kingdom still more familiar to western Europeans. From time to time it was the subject of a general appeal. The pope tried to mount a new crusade, sending encyclical letters and preachers to all parts of Europe. In his letter he usually recounted some disaster or desperate situation in Palestine, and exhorted all Christians to take part in a rescue operation. The number of occasions on which the crusade was preached in this way far exceeded the number of crusades. Vain appeals of this kind were particularly numerous in the later half of the twelfth century; investigation has shown that in the forty years between the Second Crusade and the Third they were made twice in every decade. The records show that on every occasion three elements were interconnected: first, a set-back or crisis in the East was reported by, second, a news-letter or delegation despatched from East to West to sound the alarm and to call for help, which was followed, third, by an attempt in the West to organise that help. Interconnection can be demonstrated because the second element sometimes referred explicitly to the first, while the papal letters which were part of the third often mentioned the second.[5] There is a further point of interest about these appeals which will be discussed in a later paragraph.

III

The Latin kingdom, then, was unique in its possession of the holiest places in Christendom; in the number, therefore, of its visitors from overseas; in the extent to which news of its affairs was spread far and wide; in the repeated attempts which were made to involve all Christians in its affairs. It seems not too much to say that the kingdom came to be regarded as the common responsibility of all Christians.

This point of view was urged on all Christians whenever the organisation of a new crusade was attempted, and it lay behind the development of a new form of taxation which was novel to the point of being revolutionary. In the middle years of the twelfth century European rulers took many kinds of dues and payments from various groups of their subjects, the amounts of which generally depended either on what was customary, or on what the ruler thought he could exact in the circumstances of a particular occasion. What was lacking was a tax which fell, not on this social group or that, but on the whole population and which was based on some rational method of assessment. Such a tax was first adopted in the medieval west specifically to meet the needs of the Holy Land.[6]

The year of its origin seems to have been 1166, when taxes of this kind were almost simultaneously planned, and almost certainly levied, by the kings of the French, the English and of the Latins in Jerusalem.[7] In the East extraordinary taxation was required to support Amalric's ambitious plans in Egypt.[8] Even from the time of his accession in 1162, and during the three following years, he and other magnates in Latin Syria had been sending an unusually large number of newsletters to Europe, in which the dangers besetting the crusader kingdom were explained, and many of which were addressed to Louis VII of France.[9] In 1165 Pope Alexander III issued the first general exhortation to a crusade. Both Louis VII and Henry II responded to the appeal, though not to the extent of setting out for the East. Each was far too suspicious of the other to leave his kingdom. They decided to send money to Palestine, and to raise it by the novel form of taxation to which reference has been made. It was to be assessed on income and the value of personal property, that is, of chattels as distinct from land. Its rate was to be twopence in the pound sterling in the first year, and one penny in each of the four years following. It was to be paid by the whole community. Anyone who owned a house or followed a trade, even though his goods were worth less than £1, must pay one penny.[10]

Once this form of taxation had been devised, it was used again, in the Latin kingdom in 1183, by Henry II in 1184-5, by Henry II and Philip Augustus in 1188, as part of their preparation for the Third Crusade. All these levies were specifically for the relief of the Holy Land; the reasoning behind them can presumably only have been that they must fall on all men, rich and poor, because the crusader kingdom was the responsibility of all men as Christians. If so, it can be said that the kingdom was unique not only in the ways already discussed; it was unique also in its international status.

IV

Reference has been made to a further point of interest about the appeals from East to West during the second half of the twelfth century. There was a succession of attempts by the rulers of the crusader states to involve Western monarchs in their affairs, even though this might mean submitting to Western control. As early as

1155 Raynald, prince of Antioch, had written in such terms to Louis VII. Before he had come to the East at the time of the Second Crusade, Raynald had been a minor vassal of the count of Champagne. Now he wrote to Louis begging him to deliver his principality from the dangers that threatened it. He had been born and brought up, he said, as one of Louis' men; if only the king would come to the East, Raynald would be his to command.[11] Within ten years, King Amalric was writing to Louis in similar terms. He humbly begged Louis to fulfil in deed what he had long planned in his mind, and to bring help to the Holy Land. Amalric added that he hoped for much from the Capetian and his kingdom, and that he would be ready to serve him and to submit to his commands.[12]

Appeals to the West were despatched not only by letter, but by diplomatic missions, most of them led by high-ranking ecclesiastics of the Latin kingdom. Representations were made in this way in 1168, 1169, 1171, 1173, 1180 and 1184.[13] During their course a new element entered the situation, which may have first appeared in 1169. The Annals of Cambrai report that in that year emissaries of the Latin kingdom in Paris produced to King Louis not only letters from their own monarch, but they offered him also the keys to the walled city of Jerusalem.[14]

This evidence cannot be mentioned without an expression of doubt because it is recorded only in a single source, but it receives a measure of support from the undoubted appearance of those same symbolic acts only a few years later. From 1182 to 1184 Saladin subjected the Latin kingdom to extreme military pressure. The Frankish government felt itself so direly threatened that it took appropriately drastic measures. In 1183 it levied the extraordinary tax on the personal property of its whole population to which reference has already been made.[15] In the following year a decision was taken to send to Europe a delegation more eminent and more weighty than any of its predecessors. It was to be led by the Latin patriarch of Jerusalem, the first ever to undertake the task, and he was to be accompanied by the grand masters of the two organisations which in western public opinion were most closely identified with the Holy Land, the military orders of the Hospital and the Temple.[16]

This embassy disembarked in Italy in the autumn of 1184, at a time when Frederick Barbarossa was conferring with Pope Lucius III in Verona. On 4 November the mission urged the needs of the kingdom on both Pope and Emperor. In Verona the master of the Templars died, but the patriarch and his Hospitaller colleague made a winter journey across the Alps to seek out Philip Augustus. During their series of meetings the patriarch handed the keys of Jerusalem and the Holy Sepulchre to the French king, who received and immediately returned them. Soon after the mission crossed into England. Early in February, 1185, they were in the presence of Henry II at Reading. To him they offered not only the keys, but the banner of the crusader kingdom.

How are we to interpret these gestures? Were they simply courtly expressions of deference, inviting patronage? Or were Philip and Henry being offered the kingdom and a formal invitation to assume rule there? We remember the words of Amalric to Philip's father twenty years earlier. And certainly Gerald of Wales, who tells us more than any other contemporary observer about the patriarch's visit, tells us also that he offered Henry the lordship and subjection of the kingdom, together with its fortified places, and that he did this by the unanimous wish and acclaim of the whole clergy and people.[17]

To recapitulate: the Latin kingdom was in many respects unique, and Christians in western Europe were thought to stand in a special relationship to it. From the middle years of the twelfth century onwards, it was sometimes subject to intense Muslim pressure. Its rulers repeatedly sought help from the West, especially from the pope, the emperor and the kings of England and France. They did so by means of letters, envoys and diplomatic missions. So keen were they to obtain aid that they could offer to serve, in their own kingdom, under the command of a visiting king, and were even ready, it may be, to offer such a king their kingdom.

V

There was one other method by which attempts were made to involve western rulers in the affairs of the Latin kingdom, and it was first used in those same years when the storm clouds seemed to be gathering over the kingdom, 1184 or 1185.[18] When King Amalric had died ten years earlier, he had been succeeded by his thirteen-year-old son Baldwin. It had then been known for some years that the young king was a leper, that the disease would get worse, that he would be incapable of begetting heirs, and that the kingdom would therefore pass by legitimate inheritance to one of his sisters, first to Sybil and then, if necessary, to Isabel. The choice of a husband for Sybil was therefore a momentous question for the monarchy and the kingdom. In 1176 she married William of Montferrat, a member of a leading north Italian family, related to both French and German royal houses; but he died in the following year leaving her with child, which proved to be a boy, who was also given the name Baldwin.

Sybil's second marriage in 1180 was highly controversial. Her new husband was Guy, a young Lusignan from Poitou, whom many of the baronage thought totally unsuitable to be their future king. In the 1180s, therefore, just when Saladin was pressing so hard on the kingdom, its most powerful magnates came to be sharply divided, for and against Guy.

In 1183 Guy's opponents, who had been out of office and out of favour, gained the ascendancy and the ear of the king, and at once they set themselves to exclude Sybil and Guy from the succession. They sought to achieve this in two ways. First, in 1184, they had the infant son of Sybil and William of Montferrat crowned as king in his predecessor's lifetime, so that, in the Capetian manner, there were two kings reigning simultaneously: Baldwin IV, the leper in his early twenties and Baldwin V, a child of seven. If the elder Baldwin died first, the other would be already on the throne.

The younger king, however, was also delicate. Suppose that he died too. If no other arrangements were made the crown would pass to Sybil and Guy after all. So the baronial group prevailed on Baldwin IV, in the last months of his life, to make other arrangements, and this was the second feature of the plan. If Baldwin V died before reaching his majority, a successor to him would be agreed upon by an *ad hoc* committee, consisting of the pope, the Western emperor and the kings of France and England. Once again the attempt is made to give the kingdom a special international status and to involve the top statesmen in Christendom in ordering its affairs.[19]

This ingenious exclusion device misfired. Certainly when Baldwin IV died in 1185, his nephew continued to reign; but when in turn the child died in the following year, the summit committee was never given a chance. Guy's supporters in the kingdom engineered a swift and resolute *coup d'état*. Sybil was anointed and crowned as hereditary queen; she caused Guy, her husband, to be crowned as king.

Guy then fulfilled to the hilt what his gloomiest critics had foretold. The army of Jerusalem was under his command in July, 1187 when it was annihilated by Saladin at Ḥaṭṭīn. Guy was made a prisoner and was still in Saladin's hands when the sultan took Jerusalem in the following October. Within two years the whole kingdom was lost to the Christians with two exceptions, the castle of Beaufort and the seaport town of Tyre. This last had been held by a newcomer, Conrad of Montferrat, younger brother of that William to whom reference has been made. He arrived in the Holy Land for the first time shortly after Ḥaṭṭīn, narrowly escaped capture in Muslim-held Acre and sailed a few miles up the coast to Tyre. He found it crowded with refugees and firmly took charge of a dispirited defence. Under his able leadership heavy attacks were beaten off and Tyre was saved.

In the summer of 1188 Saladin released Guy, who still bore the title of king of Jerusalem. He naturally went straight to Tyre, the only part of the kingdom and, incidentally, of the royal demesne, still in Christian hands, and demanded admission. Conrad refused to open the gates, and repeated the refusal when Guy made a second attempt in 1189. It was then that Guy, with increasing support, went southwards down the coast road and, in the last week of August, sat down to besiege Acre. So began one of the major episodes of the Third Crusade.

The Muslims did not surrender Acre until July, 1191; the siege begun by Guy had lasted only six weeks less than two years. During its course, in October 1190, Queen Sybil had died. What was Guy's position then? Did he remain king because he had been crowned, or did the hereditary right of succession pass to Sybil's half-sister Isabel? It hardly needs to be said that Guy adopted the first point of view, while Conrad emphasised the importance of the second by promptly marrying Isabel, brushing aside the obstacle that both were married already. So that the complications of the crusade were further complicated by a disputed succession.

VI

The recital of a familiar narrative in the preceding section clears the ground for carrying the main subject-matter of this paper a further step forward.

When Conrad was refusing Guy admission into Tyre, contemporaries offered more than one interpretation of his motives. Some believed that he claimed possession of the city because its inhabitants had received him as their lord;[20] or because God had given it to him;[21] or because it had been entrusted to him so that he could restore it 'to the king and the heirs of the kingdom'.[22] But Saladin's judge of the army, Bahā' al-Dīn Ibn Shaddād, who was in southern Syria at the material time, and an annalist of Genoa, some of whose merchants were always in close touch with the affairs of the Latin East, had both heard that Conrad was acting as 'the lieutenant of the kings beyond the seas',[23] and that Tyre had been 'placed in his custody until the arrival of one of the four crowned heads, namely, of the Emperor Frederick, of the king of the French or of England, or of the Lord William, king of Sicily.'[24] In other words, a view was being expressed by some contemporaries that the right to dispose of the city lay with the rulers of the West, on whose behalf Conrad was holding it as a kind of trustee. The Latin kingdom was not fully autonomous and its affairs were ultimately a Western responsibility.

This element became still more pronounced as the rivalry between Conrad and Guy intensified. Both of them saw an opportunity to gain support when, at long last, the kings of France and England arrived in the eastern Mediterranean to join the final stages of the siege of Acre. Conrad was a kinsman of Philip Augustus and soon moved in his orbit, but Guy was not to be outdone. His family were Richard's vassals in Poitou, so it is not surprising to find him eager to make contact with the king, so eager that he, with a number of his supporters, took ship to meet Richard in Cyprus, before ever that monarch had reached the Holy Land. There, we are told by Howden, who was himself on crusade, 'they offered the king their service, and became his men, and swore fealty to him against all men'.[25] So Guy, a crowned king of Jerusalem, who claimed that his title was as strong as it had ever been, became in due form a vassal of King Richard, and in the months that followed, Richard dealt with him as a good lord should. He supported Guy's claim to retain the crown of Jerusalem and, at the last, when his vassal's cause became hopeless, compensated him with Cyprus. So, in this way also, a Western ruler was brought into the affairs of the Latin kingdom.

One last episode. Later in that same summer an attempt was made to impose a solemn and final solution on the disputed succession. In late July, 1191, in the days which followed the crusader conquest of Acre, Conrad and Guy formally submitted their claims before Philip Augustus and Richard, sitting together in judgement. After protracted argument and counter-argument, a formal verdict was duly given. Guy was to remain king during his lifetime, but no progeny of his should have the right to succeed. After Guy, the succession should pass to Conrad, Isabel and their heirs.[26] The descent of the Latin kingdom was thus settled in 1191 by procedures which somewhat resembled those envisaged six years earlier. Had Barbarossa survived the journey to the East, he would no doubt have presided over the court at Acre, and would thus have made the resemblance still closer. The settlement included one other significant feature. If Guy, Conrad and Isabel were all to die while Richard was still in the Holy Land, then he should dispose of the kingdom by his sole decision.[27]

VII

Thus far the international status of the Latin kingdom has been discussed mainly in the light of initiatives taken in the East to involve Western rulers in the kingdom's affairs. There is another side to the coin, and it is represented by that series of occasions when Western magnates from outside the kingdom, apparently without any prompting, behaved as if they had special rights there.

Conrad of Montferrat provides a spectacular starting point. As already stated, he was a newcomer to the East in the summer of 1187 and at once assumed responsibility for the defence of Tyre. As early as October 1187, months before Guy was released from captivity and presented himself before the gates of Tyre, Conrad was beginning to behave as if he were lord of that city. In particular, he made extensive grants of commercial privileges to the Pisans, who were giving outstanding service in the defence of Tyre.[28]

To put this matter in perspective, the merchants of Genoa, Pisa and Venice very highly prized their commercial bases in the crusader states, and especially the right to trade in privileged conditions in places like Acre and Tyre. They had gained such rights by the essential naval help they had given in the early years of the twelfth century, which had enabled the first Latin kings of Jerusalem to reduce the all-important coastal places. In return the Italians had received commercial privileges, and nearly all these grants, certainly the most important of them, had been made by the kings of Jerusalem. Saladin's conquests in 1187 and 1188 had meant the loss of all those places in the kingdom, save one, in which those privileges had been exercised. The Italians therefore had a major stake in any new crusade, since this represented the best way of getting their privileges back.

Conrad, therefore, in taking the lead in restoring those privileges, was assuming powers normally exercised by the kings of Jerusalem. And he went a good deal further along the same road when he began to grant such rights not only in Tyre, which he could after all claim that he had saved from capture, but in Acre and Jaffa as well.[29] In Acre he had never set foot; on Jaffa he had never set eye; in neither did he possess a shred of legal right.

This example of a magnate from outside the kingdom behaving as if he possessed, or had acquired, special rights there, was often to be repeated. In order to transport to Acre his following of 650 knights, each with two squires and two horses, Philip Augustus made a contract with the Genoese, who agreed to provide the necessary shipping and stores for a fixed sum. As part of the terms Philip also agreed that in all lands conquered by him and his barons the Genoese should have the right to trade free of all entry and exit charges; that in all towns taken by the French which had formerly been in Frankish possession, the Genoese should recover any rights they had held there and that in all new conquests they should be given a street with warehouses, a bakery and baths.[30] These clauses clearly envisaged the possibility of Philip exercising rights in the Latin kingdom which had previously belonged to the Latin kings. And Richard was to do so in fact, since in October, 1191 he confirmed to the Pisans everything that Guy had granted them in the kingdom.[31]

Philip and Richard were to provide, between them, a still more striking example of the take-over of royal power within the territories of the kingdom. Before they set out on crusade they agreed to divide whatever gains they made during the expedition. When Acre was regained, they put their agreement into operation, and each occupied half the city. When Philip left the Holy Land to return to France, he gave his half to Conrad of Montferrat.[32] During the year that elapsed before his own departure from Palestine, Richard played the leading part in the kingdom's affairs. It was recognised by all groups concerned in the politics of the country, whether they were his opponents or supporters, that any solution to the problem of the succession, if it was to be stable, needed his consent.

VIII

In a comment on an earlier paper by the present writer, Professor Mayer remarked that the subject matter was 'bequem zusammengestellt, nach der Rechtsgrundlage freilich nicht untersucht.'[33] The same position has been reached again. Evidence has been assembled to illustrate the singular international status of the Latin kingdom of Jerusalem. Did this rest on any legal foundations or on general principles of any kind? Mayer's comment assumed, and in his paper he argued, that such foundations existed. Before discussing this aspect of the matter further, however, it is important to notice how large a part was played by the urgent short-term requirements of particular diplomatic and political situations. Most of the pieces of evidence which have been brought together in the foregoing sections of this article were the product of such conditions.

IX

The years between the Second and the Third Crusades saw the balance of power in Syria between the Franks and the Muslims changing to the detriment of the Franks. 'Ab ea die coepit Orientalium Latinorum manifeste deterior fieri conditio.'[34] Thus

William of Tyre, reflecting on the failure of the Second Crusade and its consequences, and the deterioration continued as the position of the Syrian Muslims became still stronger. In the 1150s Nūr al-Dīn completed his father's achievement in Syria by acquiring Damascus, its natural capital, in the 1160s he added Egypt to Syria. In the 1170s Saladin, from a power base in Egypt, was able to occupy most of Syria after Nūr al-Dīn's death; in the 1180s he completed that occupation by the acquisition of Aleppo and extended his power into the lands beyond the Euphrates. With ever-increasing human and material resources at his disposal, he was able to intensify his pressure on the crusader states.

In these circumstances the Franks felt a growing need for Christian help from outside their own borders. In the third quarter of the twelfth century they strengthened their diplomatic ties with Byzantium and they also made repeated approaches to Western rulers. They wanted a European king, preferably Louis VII, to lead an expedition to the Holy Land. But if Louis, or any other monarch, were to come to the East, what would be his position in the Latin kingdom, especially in relation to the Latin king? There was a possible source of difficulty here; but since the king of Jerusalem was a petitioner who was begging a favour, and since he came to know how very difficult it was to induce any Western ruler to undertake the long and expensive journey, and to leave his kingdom exposed to external enemies and domestic troublemakers, he was prepared to defer to a visitor for whose help he felt so urgent a need. And when after 1174, with the advent of Saladin, that need became still more pressing, and when the Latin king was first a minor, and then a leper beyond hope of cure, then he and his advisers were prepared to defer to a western visitor to the point of putting him in charge of the government.

This hypothesis is supported by verifiable evidence. We have not only King Amalric's assurances in letters which he sent to Louis VII in 1163 and 1164 that he would be subject to the Capetian if he came to the Holy Land,[35] but we have the readiness of King Baldwin IV, with the full agreement of his episcopal and baronial advisers, to put the government of the kingdom into the hands of Philip of Alsace, count of Flanders, when the count came on pilgrimage to Jerusalem in 1177. In his great history of the Latin kingdom, William of Tyre recorded a number of occasions on which, because of the king's absence or incapacity, the government was put in charge of a regent. Such a responsibility was given to Eustace Garnier in 1122, while Baldwin II was a prisoner in Muslim hands; to Fulk and Melisende, son-in-law and daughter of that same king when, in 1131, nearing his end, he wished to relinquish power; to Raymond of Tripoli in 1174, during the minority of Baldwin IV; to Guy of Lusignan and then to Raymond again, in 1183, when that king was too ill to discharge his duties. To these instances may be added Baldwin II's temporary assumption of power in Antioch after Prince Roger's death in battle in 1119. In recording such temporary transfers of power William, as befitted a chancellor of the kingdom, was entirely consistent in his vocabulary.[36] In describing the offer made to the count of Flanders, however, he set out its terms in greater detail than can be found in any comparable passage, and his words merit particular attention not only because of the high office he held, but because of the leading part he played in the negotiations with Philip.[37] It was proposed that the count should be in full charge of the government, and it was further spelt out that his authority was to be effective both in peace and war and in the all-important fields of jurisdiction and finance. The whole transaction makes it abundantly clear that certainly there were circumstances in which the king of Jerusalem and his greatest subjects were prepared to hand over the government of the kingdom to a magnate from the West. It is clear furthermore that, whatever degree of consideration the magnates of the kingdom may have given to legal or theoretical principles when debating whether to invite a stranger to take over the government, they were certainly and strongly influenced by the contemporary political and military situation.

In the early 1180s the king's physical condition still further deteriorated, while Saladin's attacks on the kingdom grew ever more threatening. The problem of finding an effective head of government therefore took on a new urgency. Attempts in 1183 to appoint first Guy of Lusignan and then Raymond of Tripoli divided the magnates of the kingdom. The search was therefore renewed in Europe, and reference has been made already to the mission of 1184-5 led by the patriarch and the masters of the military orders. Their dramatic offer of the keys and the banner of Jerusalem to two of the most powerful kings of the West symbolised not only the desperate needs of the kingdom, but a readiness to hand over the direction of the government, perhaps even the crown itself.[38]

The repeated and increasingly urgent attempts to involve European monarchs in the affairs of the kingdom of Jerusalem arose directly and in large part from that kingdom's domestic and external problems. Irrespective of whether such involvement rested on a theoretical basis, it was pursued as a necessary and practical solution to visible and pressing dangers.

X

The domestic problems of the kingdom crystallised into an exclusion crisis and a succession dispute, both sharpened by personal animosities. Guy of Lusignan's opponents attached such importance to denying him succession to the throne in the right of his wife, Sybil, that they first arranged for the coronation of Sybil's infant son by her first marriage and then, in the event of the death of that child before he had begotten heirs, for the succession to be decided by the pope, the emperor and the kings of France and England. This introduction of a team of external potentates into the affairs of the kingdom, so far from being in accordance with any known legal considerations, was an astute tactical move, devised in the course of an all-out political battle, for setting aside the normal laws of succession. In 1186 Guy and his supporters were able to secure the operation of those laws, so that he and Sybil became king and queen. It was under their rule that the kingdom was virtually lost to Saladin in the aftermath of Ḥaṭṭīn, and of its towns only Tyre was saved to the Franks by the timely arrival of Conrad of Montferrat.

Conrad, ambitious and without scruple, was prepared to play a hard political game. When Guy was released from captivity, Conrad shut him out of Tyre, made grants to the Italian merchants in the manner of the former kings of Jerusalem and was soon making public references to Guy as a man who had 'once been king'.[39] The direction of Conrad's ambition was clear: he intended to become king of Jerusalem himself. On what did he base his claim? Can it be said that it was 'by the most absolute right of possession then known, the right of conquest'?[40] To put the matter in this way may seem to give the situation a legal character which it did not in fact possess. To Conrad, at all events, the advantage which the successful defence of Tyre gave him was less a source of law or right than a card in his hand to be played or withheld according to the state of the game.

When Guy could not secure admission to Tyre, he moved down the coast, in late August 1189, to form the siege of Acre. By this bold stroke he took the initiative from his opponent. Conrad had been preserving the last remnant of the kingdom; Guy now began the work of winning the kingdom back. He gained increasing support, not only from newly arrived crusaders, but also from some of his former opponents among the baronage of the kingdom. Even by November 1189 Guy's charters, in which he used his royal title, were being witnessed by Balian of Ibelin and by Raymond of Tripoli's stepsons, Hugh and William of Tiberias.[41] By the spring of 1190 the Jerusalemite group of witnesses was increased still further by Count Joscelin the seneschal and at last, *mirabile dictu*, by Conrad himself, witnessing as lord of Tyre.[42] At that stage, it will be noted, he was no longer claiming rights of conquest, except possibly in respect of Tyre. He had been persuaded to act with Guy, and even to recognise him as king.

In the autumn of 1190 the situation was once more changed, and changed drastically, by the death of Queen Sybil, which deprived Guy of the major source of his right to be accepted as king. Since Sybil' daughters by Guy had predeceased her, it was widely accepted that the title now passed by hereditary descent to her young half-sister Isabel, whom Conrad, seizing his opportunity, promptly married.[43] It was yet another change of tactics. The marquis was now preparing to base a claim to the crown on the rights inherited by his wife, rights of a kind he had been prepared to set aside when they had been in favour of Sybil and Guy.

The leading barons of Jerusalem, who accepted Isabel as the legitimate heir, now transferred their support to Conrad. The earliest surviving charter which he issued with *domina Isabella, uxor eius* was witnessed by Balian of Ibelin, Raynald of Sidon and Pagan of Haifa.[44] In the next, dated 7 May 1191, these have been joined by Hugh of Tiberias. By this date Philip Augustus had arrived in Palestine and had immediately given his support to

Conrad. Thus fortified by the accession of three fresh sources of support in eight months - a wife, major barons and a king - it is not surprising to find that in his charter of 7 May Conrad has taken the all-important step of styling himself *rex Jerosolimorum electus*.[45] Exactly a month later King Richard landed at Acre, having already met Guy in Cyprus, accepted his homage and given him support. So that the situation was wide open again until the compromise judgement given by the two kings in late July. Even this settled nothing. Philip continued to support Conrad until the day of his departure from Palestine; for example, he gave the half of Acre he controlled not to Guy, the agreed king, as might have been expected, but to Conrad.[46] Still supported by the leading figures of the baronage of Jerusalem, Conrad continued to do everything possible to undermine the authority of Richard and to erode the position of Guy. And he succeeded. Early in 1192 Richard was forced to recognise that Guy, his protégé, no longer commanded adequate support in the kingdom and that there was, on the contrary, overwhelming support for Conrad. If Conrad had not been murdered in the streets of Acre in April, 1192, he would have been crowned king of Jerusalem with Richard's consent.

It has been said already that part of the Latin kingdom's unique character was illustrated by a 'series of occasions when Western magnates from outside the kingdom, apparently without any prompting, behaved as if they had special rights there.'[47] Conrad of Montferrat was one such magnate. He was no man of principle. His activities in the kingdom through a period of nearly five years were directed towards acquiring the crown, and to achieve this he was prepared to use any tactical advantage, as opportunity served. Of those advantages, the right of conquest was one, which sometimes he used, and sometimes not.

XI

Does the conduct of Philip Augustus and Richard as crusaders help towards an understanding of the international status of the Latin kingdom? They, too, have been regarded as exponents of the rights of conquest.[48] Importance has been attached to the agreement they made before they left Vézélay together that they would divide between them any profits or conquests they made while on crusade. It has seemed to some historians that they were thereby ignoring the very existence of the Latin kingdom and its monarchy.[49]

The matter may not be quite so straightforward. It has to be observed at the outset that we do not know precisely what they agreed. Of a number of contemporary ordinances and treaties we have either a text or a detailed description of their contents by well-informed observers; of the kings' agreement to divide what they won by military action we have neither.[50] Did it cover the profits of war normal to that age, like plunder and ransoms, or was it to be applied to territorial conquests? Since the two kings subsequently divided the prisoners taken in Acre,[51] and Philip claimed half of the island of Cyprus after its conquest by

Richard,[52] the agreement presumably covered both profits and conquests, but it may be noted that our uncertainty about the exact terms of their compact seems to have been shared at times by the kings themselves. Philip's claim to Cyprus, for example, was rejected by Richard on the grounds that he supposed their agreement to be valid only in the land of Jerusalem.[53]

The purpose of the kings in making this agreement was not simply to declare an attitude to the Latin kingdom and its rulers. The disposal of the conquests made by crusaders was already an old and recurrent problem in crusading history, of which it was sensible to take account in planning any new expedition. From the very beginning of the First Crusade the Byzantine emperor Alexius Comnenus had acutely perceived the difficulties and had exerted himself to exact an oath from the leaders of the expedition that they would return to him any place they reconquered which had once been part of the East Roman Empire.[54] But this arrangement could not prevent the crisis and the longstanding dispute that arose over the disposal of Antioch.

Fifty years later the siege of Damascus by the forces of the Second Crusade foundered on many disagreements: among them was the problem as to whom among the Franks the city should be given if it were conquered. Some of the barons of the Latin kingdom strongly resented the possibility that it might go to a newcomer from the West, and this resentment weakened their commitment to the siege.[55]

This old problem had become no easier when the Third Crusade was being organised, but represented a possible source of future difficulty which Philip and Richard could hardly ignore. In planning the crusade it was particularly important to establish conditions in which the two kings could work together, and from which all causes for dispute had as far as possible been removed. Given the recurrent discords and hostilities between them and between their fathers in the past, what likelier cause for conflict than disposal of the profits of war? Far better to preserve the mutuality which marked the treaty they concluded in March, 1190 and to agree to a division.[56]

A possible alternative was to hand conquests over to the king of Jerusalem. But who was the king of Jerusalem? When Philip and Richard took the Cross, Guy was in captivity and his fate still uncertain. When they arrived at Acre they found an unresolved dispute about the crown, with Guy using the royal title and Conrad formally describing himself as king of Jerusalem elect. In such a situation, to whom should they have handed over Acre when it surrendered? Again, better for them to occupy it jointly, each taking possession of one half, until the affair of the kingdom could be settled. Their decision was bitterly resented by crusaders who had borne the dangers and privations of the siege for much longer than the kings and their followers.[57] In other words, when the kings divided Acre they were not acting in accordance with any recognisable law or right which everyone accepted. They were using their superior force to impose a temporary solution which no-one could resist, and it is not easy to see what else they could have done in the moment of victory.

Furthermore, were not Philip and Richard behaving in ways which earlier Latin kings had urged on their fathers? Letters and envoys from Jerusalem had besought and exhorted Louis VII and Henry II to come on crusade. They were asked, when they came to the East, to take charge there; the rulers of Latin Syria would serve and obey them. The message was emphasised on important occasions by the symbolic offer of visible objects. They had been asked to do what Philip and Richard in fact did: to come to the Latin kingdom and to take charge in operations against the Muslims. In the circumstances of 1191, could they have done otherwise? Under whose command could they conceivably have placed themselves? It seems hard to conclude that they showed contempt for the rulers of the Latin kingdom or that they departed from ideas already developed in the past.

XII

The factual evidence for the special international status of the crusader kingdom in the second half of the twelfth century was reviewed in sections II to VII of this paper. In sections IX to XI it has been shown that many of the events and ideas which constitute the facts came into existence as the result of some of the urgent short-term needs of the kingdom and of the changes and chances of its internal politics. Were there no larger, long-range forces at work?

Professor Mayer believes that the powers ascribed to European rulers in the affairs of the Latin kingdom, and which were sometimes exercised there, demand a theoretical explanation; they could not have arisen in a vacuum of constitutional law. He has suggested that they may ultimately have derived from beliefs which had their roots in the Carolingian period. When the patriarch of Jerusalem sent Charlemagne the keys and the banner of Jerusalem, it is likely that he intended these symbols to mark no more than his honour and respect; but there were Franks who came to believe that the patriarch was thereby recognising Charlemagne's authority in the Holy Land. In the twelfth century, when a variety of royal persons showed themselves aware of the importance of their Carolingian heritage, were these supposed rights of Charlemagne in Palestine regarded as having passed to the rulers of the Carolingian successor states and so to the Capetians and the Western emperors, even to the Angevin rulers of England and Normandy?[58]

This brilliant suggestion needs, as its author recognises, further examination and discussion. All that is attempted here is to place another suggestion beside it. It goes back to the second and third sections of this paper, where it was noted that the Latin kingdom was widely regarded as the special possession and responsibility of Western Christendom as a whole. This viewpoint was clearly adopted in the preaching of the crusade throughout the twelfth century. The appeals which were made for these expeditions to the East were not drafted in terms of organising help for a king or a kingdom, nor was the expeditionary force envisaged as a regularly constituted feudal or mercenary army recruited by a western government. Encyclicals and sermons commonly referred instead to the needs of Christendom as a whole and they often spoke to all Christians who accepted the authority of Rome. The information they disseminated about Near-Eastern affairs was not cast in terms of current politics, but of the land in which Christ had lived and taught as a man, *ubi steterunt pedes eius*, and the threat not specifically of Muslim, but of heathen conquest to which it was exposed. Western Christians were told how the places made holy by his death and resurrection, which had been won back from the heathen by the heroism and self-sacrifice of earlier generations of Latin Christians, were once again in danger of defilement by unbelievers. Such a tragedy would dishonour the Christian name and would be an insult to Christ himself, who by shedding his blood in that land redeemed mankind. Let Christians repay the debt and render the service they owe him by undertaking the journey to the Lord's land and by fighting in its defence. Those who played a part in such holy work were assured of rich rewards. They earned remission of the penance imposed for sin both in this world and in purgatory; some could believe that they received full absolution from sin and all its consequences, or that they won the crown of everlasting life. And all were told that by taking the Cross they were fulfilling the most stringent demands of Christ himself and were thus exhibiting a degree of devotion to their religion which could not possibly be exceeded. 'If any man will come after me, let him deny himself, and take up his Cross and follow me.'[59] Expression was given to all these ideas at the time of the First Crusade;[60] they were powerfully developed in the letters and treatises of Saint Bernard at the time of the Second,[61] repeated in papal encyclicals issued between the Second and the Third,[62] and spilled over into the poetry of the day, both Latin and vernacular.

As a result of appeals made in these terms the leading figures in a major crusade found themselves at the head of a large concentration of pilgrims, sent to defend or conquer a land solely because of its special significance for all Christians, from peoples who were regarded as enemies solely because they were pagans. It was not the territory of a friendly ally, but a land in which no Christian could be a foreigner and for which he had a direct responsibility. Europeans were induced to campaign there from Christian considerations: they would be obeying Christ's commands to the limit and would be earning the highest rewards to which a Christian could aspire. Small wonder that the leaders of such an undertaking which so far transcended local and secular considerations should act as those from whom was due no deference to local and secular authorities, not even to a crowned king of Jerusalem. The problem remained to add to the difficulties of crusaders in the thirteenth century.

R. C. SMAIL

1. R. C. Smail, 'Latin Syria and the West, 1149-1187', *Transactions of the Royal Historical Society*, 5th series, 19, 1969, 1-20. Cited hereafter as Smail, with page reference.

2. H. E. Mayer, 'Kaiserrecht und Heiliges Land', *Aus Reichsgeschichte und Nordischer Geschichte*, Kieler Historische Studien, 1972, 193-208. Cited hereafter as Mayer, with page reference.

3. Mayer, 208.

4. J. P. Migne, *Patrologia Latina* (=*P. L.*) 200, col.1294.

5. Smail, 19.

6. A. Cartellieri, *Philipp II August*, II, Leipzig and Paris, 1906, 85. 'Aus den Nöten des heiligen Landes, die alles, was Christ heisst, in Mitleidenschaft ziehen, entsteht moderne Steuergesetzgebung.'

7. B. Z. Kedar, 'The general tax of 1183 in the crusading kingdom of Jerusalem: innovation or adaptation?', *English Historical Review*, LXXXIX, 1974, 339-45, adduces evidence that the tax was in fact collected by the French and English kings. See especially p.343. Neither he nor S. K. Mitchell, *Taxation in medieval England*, Yale, 1951, 114-17 has any doubt on that point.

8. William of Tyre, *Historia rerum in partibus transmarinis gestarum, Recueil des Historiens des Croisades*, (=*R.H.C*), *Historiens Occidentaux* (=*Hist. Occ.*), I, Paris, 1844, 903.

9. For a fuller discussion of the contents of the rest of this paragraph, Smail, 8-12.

10. Mitchell, *op.cit.*, 114; Kedar, *op.cit.*, 340-43.

11. R. Röhricht, *Regesta regni hierosolymitani*, Innsbruck, 1893 (=*Regesta*), and *Additamentum*, Innsbruck, 1904, no.319; M. Bouquet, *Receuil des historiens des Gaules et de la France* (=*R.H.G.F*), XVI, Paris, 1878, 15. '...ad jussum vestrum adimplendum paratus sum.'

12. *Regesta*, no.382; *R.H.G.F.*, XVI, 59. 'Quoniam vestram personam et regnum vestrum diligimus, et vobis servire parati sumus, et specialiter de vobis et de regno vestro speramus...' *Regesta*, no.394; *R.H.G.F.*, XVI, 40. '...quia non in terram alienam, verum in eam quae in omnibus et per omnia vobis erit exposita, venietis; et tam nos, quam omnes alii, jussionibus vestris obtemperabimus.'

13. Smail, 13-9.

14. *Annales Cameracenses*, in *Monumenta Germaniae Historica* (=*M.G.H*), *Scriptores*, xvi, 1859, 550.

15. William of Tyre, 1109-12.

16. Mayer, 203-06; Cartellieri, *op. cit*, II, 18-25.

17. Giraldus Cambrensis, *Opera*, (ed. G. F. Warner), VIII, Rolls Series, 1891, 203. '...totius tam cleri quam populi unanimi voto et acclamatione regni dominium cum castellis quoque, quae ante petierat, eidem obtulit et subiectionem.'

18. The subject matter of this section is made familiar by the accounts given in all histories of the crusades. See, for example, Mayer, *The Crusades*, Oxford, 1972, 128-33, 139-41 or Runciman, *History of the Crusades*, Cambridge, 1951-54, II, 423-73; III, 19-31.

19. *L'estoire de Eracles Empereur* (=*Eracles*), *R.H.C.*, *Hist.Occ.*, II, 7; *Chronique d'Ernoul et de Bernard le Trésorier* (ed. M. L. de Mas Latrie), Paris, 1871, 117.

20. *Eracles*, *R.H.C.*, *Hist.Occ.*, II, 125.

21. *Eracles*, *R.H.C.*, *Hist.Occ.*, II, 124; *Chronique d'Ernoul*, 257.

22. *Das Itinerarium peregrinorum* (ed. H. E. Mayer), Stuttgart, 1962, 305.

23. Bahā' al-Dīn Ibn Shaddād, *al-Nawādir al-sulṭāniyya wa'l-maḥāsin al-Yūsufiyya* (ed. Gamal el-Din el-Shayyal), [Cairo] 1964, 98; (tr. C. W. Wilson and C. R. Conder); *The life of Saladin*, Library of the Palestine Pilgrims' Text Society, XIII, London, 1897, 144.

24. *Annali Genovesi di Caffaro e de' suoi continuatori* (ed. L. T. Belgrano), I, Rome, 1890, 145.

25. Roger of Howden, *Chronica* (ed. W. Stubbs), III, Rolls Series, 1870, 108.

26. Howden, *Chronica*, III, 124; Ambroise, *L'Estoire de la Guerre Sainte* (=*Estoire*) (ed. G. Paris), Paris, 1897, Collection des documents inédits sur l'histoire de France, lines 5041-64; *Itinerarium peregrinorum et gesta regis Ricardi* (ed. W. Stubbs), Rolls Series, 1864, 235-36.

27. There is a lacuna at this important point in the unique MS.

of the *Estoire*. See line 5063 and the editor's comment on p.388, note 1. The detail about Richard is supplied by the almost contemporary Latin translation, in *Itinerarium* (ed. Stubbs), 236.

28. *Regesta*, no.665; text in *Documenti sulle relazioni delle città toscane coll'Oriente cristiano e coi Turchi fino all' anno 1531*, (ed. G. Müller), Documenti degli archivi toscani, 3, Florence, 1879, no.XXIII, 26-8.

29. *Regesta*, nos.667, 668; *Documenti*, (ed. Müller), nos.XXIV, XXV, 28-31.

30. *Liber iurium reipublicae Genuensis*, *Historiae patriae monumenta*, VII, Turin, 1854, no.372, 355-56.

31. *Regesta*, no.706; *Documenti*, (ed. Müller), no.XXXV, 58-9.

32. Howden, *Chronica*, III, 125.

33. Mayer, 199.

34. William of Tyre, 771.

35. See note 12 above.

36. William of Tyre, 538 (*sub anno* 1122): tradunt ei curam regni et administrationem generalem. 602 (1131): tradidit eis curam regni et plenam potestatem. 1010 (1174): tradita est ei universa procuratio et potestas regni. 1116 (1183): constituit Guidonem procuratorem regni. Contulit ei generalem et liberam administrationem. 1134 (1183): committit ei curam regni et generalem administrationem.

37. William of Tyre, 1027: obtulit ei potestatem et liberam et generalem administrationem super regnum universum, ut et in pace et in guerra, intus et foris super majores et minores plenam haberet jurisdictionem, et ut super thesauros et reditus regni libere exerceret arbitrium suum.

38. Mayer, 204-06, argues persuasively that the patriarch went to Europe to find a king who would replace the existing royal house in Jerusalem, and that in this project he had the support of what was probably a majority of the secular and ecclesiastical magnates of the Latin kingdom. The offering of the keys and the banner symbolised an offering of the crown. The patriarch and his companions were certainly looking for someone to take charge of the government in Jerusalem, but it seems less certain that they were planning the deposition of the reigning dynasty. Mayer accepts that the keys of Jerusalem had been produced in Paris by a mission from the

East in 1169. At three places in his text (206, 208) he couples this occasion with the symbolic acts of Heraclius in 1184-5. There can surely have been no plan in 1169 to remove the crown from so vigorous and masterful a king as Amalric; and if the offer of the keys did not betoken a deposition in 1169, why should it have done so in 1185?

39. In a letter to the Archbishop of Canterbury. *Regesta*, no.676; Ralph of Diceto, *Ymagines historiarum*, (ed. W. Stubbs), II, Rolls Series, 1876, 60-2. See especially 61: Et quia Tyrum conservavi et conservo, Guidoni de Lisigniaco quondam regi ... molestum est et inportabile.

40. Jonathan Riley-Smith, *The feudal nobility and the kingdom of Jerusalem, 1174-1277*, London, 1973, 113.

41. *Regesta*, no.683; Müller, *Documenti*, no.XXXI, 36-8.

42. *Regesta*, no.693; *Liber iurium*, *H.P.M.*, VII, no.375, 360.

43. *Das Itinerarium peregrinorum*, (ed. Mayer), 354-5.

44. *Regesta*, no.703; Müller, *Documenti*, no.XXXIII, 39-40.

45. *Regesta*, no.705; *Urkunden zur ältern Handels - und Staatsgeschichte der Republik Venedig mit besonderer Beziehung auf Byzanz und die Levante*, (ed. G.L.F. Tafel and G. M. Thomas), 3 vols. Vienna, 1856-7, I, no.76, 212-15.

46. Note 32 above.

47. See p.30 above.

48. Riley-Smith, *Feudal Nobility*, 113.

49. J. Prawer, *The Latin kingdom of Jerusalem*, London, 1972, 107. 'Richard ... and Philip ... agreed to divide their future conquests, as if no political and legitimate power existed in the realm.'

50. It seems that we cannot get closer to it than the brief, general statement by Ambroise, *Estoire*, lines 369-70.

51. Howden, *Chronica*, III, 125.

52. Howden, *Chronica*, III, 114.

53. *ibid.*

54. Anna Comnena, *Alexiad*, X, 9; (ed. B. Leib), 226; F.-L. Ganshof 'Recherche sur le lien juridique qui unissait les chefs de la

première croisade à l'empereur byzantin', *Mélanges offerts à M. Paul-E. Martin*, Geneva, 1961, 51 and n.3, 59, 61.

55. William of Tyre,• 768-9.

56. Howden, *Chronica*, II, 144-46; III, 30-1. The editor of the *Chronica* dates the second of these treaties to January 1190. This should be corrected to March 1190, as shown by L. Landon, *The Itinerary of King Richard I*, Publications of the Pipe Roll Society, new series, XIII, 1935, 27.

57. Howden, *Chronica*, III, 123.

58. Mayer, 206-08.

59. *Gesta Francorum et aliorum Hierosolimitanorum* (ed. Rosalind Hill), London, 1962, 1; Innocent III's encyclical *Quia Major* (1213), *P. L.*, 216, coll.817.

60. P. Rousset, *Les origines et les caractères de la Première Croisade*, Neuchâtel, 1945, 68-109.

61. Rousset, *op. cit.*, 152-68; E. Delaruelle, 'L'idée de croisade chez saint Bernard', *Mélanges saint Bernard*, Dijon, 1953, 53-67.

62. See particularly the major papal letters of the period relating to the crusade; *Quantum predecessores* (1165), *P. L.*, 200, coll.384-86; *Inter omnia* (1169), *P. L.*, 200, coll.599-601; *Cum gemitus* (1169), *P. L.*, 200, coll.601-02; *Non sine gravi dolore* (1173-74), *P. L.*, 200, coll.927-28; *Ingemiscimus et dolemus* (1173-74), *Gulielmi Neubrigensis historia ... libris quinque*, (ed. T. Hearne), III, Oxford, 1719, 664; *Cum orientalis terra* (1181), *Gesta regis Henrici II* (=*Gesta*) (ed. W. Stubbs), I, Rolls Series, 1867, 275; *Cor nostrum* (1181), *Gesta*, I, 272-74; *Cum cuncti predecessores* (1185), *Gesta*, I, 332-33.

The structure of government in the Mamluk sultanate

The Mamluk sultan was an autocrat with arbitrary discretion but technically he was neither absolute nor sovereign. As a Muslim he was bound by the Holy Law of Islam as much as any of his subjects, although in practice its judges lacked sanctions which they could enforce against him. Islamic doctrine, as expounded by Sunnī jurists, knew of only one sovereign (under God) over the Muslim community, namely the caliph. Hence the physical extinction of the ʿAbbasid caliphate by Hülegü in 656/1258 created an unprecedented situation. It was formally rectified in 659/1261, when the Mamluk sultan, al-Ẓāhir Baybars, received in Egypt a refugee ʿAbbasid prince and caused him to be installed as caliph with the throne-name of al-Mustanṣir. Following practice going back to the time of the Prophet, the caliph as head of the Muslim community received an oath of recognition from Baybars, to whom in turn he delegated his authority over the Islamic lands and future conquests from the unbelievers. This magnificently staged ceremony (which was repeated in 661/1262, after al-Mustanṣir's death in battle and the selection of another ʿAbbasid) was not merely a pompous charade; three important objectives were attained thereby. One was legal: the interregnum was over, the lawyers could feel confident that the decisions of judges were valid and that marriages were lawfully contracted. The other two objectives were political. The Mamluk sultanate had begun by usurpation from the Ayyubids and Baybars himself had come to the throne by murdering his predecessor. The caliph's diploma now gave him a basis of legitimacy for his rule. Furthermore it recognised him not merely as sultan in Egypt and Syria, the territories which he actually ruled, but as the universal sultan, the caliph's delegate throughout the Islamic lands and those still held by the unbelievers. This proclaimed and consecrated in advance a programme of expansion at the expense of other rulers, whether Muslim, such as the remaining Ayyubids, or infidel, that is specifically the Frankish rulers and the Mongol *īl-khān*.

The participation of the caliph in the inauguration of a new sultan continued throughout the Mamluk period. His delegation of plenary powers was manifested in two ways. First, as part of the accession observances, the sultan put on a black robe, the livery of the ʿAbbasid dynasty. The texts make it clear that in many instances the sultan was actually invested with this robe *(al-khilʿa al-khalīfatiyya)* by the caliph. Secondly, the caliph (not invariably) declared in express terms his recognition of the sultan, sometimes by a written diploma *(taqlīd* or *ʿahd)*, following the precedent set by al-Mustanṣir. In the time of the late Qalawunids, however, there appears another form of conferment of the sultanate, by *bayʿa*, i.e. formal profession of recognition. This seems anomalous, since the *bayʿa* was traditionally given by subjects to the caliph as head of the Islamic community, or to the sultan as his delegate, but the *bayʿa* from the caliph to the sultan seems curiously to reverse their constitutional positions. Nevertheless, the formula 'the caliph made the *bayʿa* to him upon the sultanate' *(bāyaʿahu al-khalīfa bi'l-salṭana)* appears occasionally from the accession of al-Nāṣir Aḥmad (742/1342) to the end of the Qalawunid dynasty, and becomes usual with al-Ẓāhir Barqūq and the Circassian sultans. It is significant that when the last of the Qalawunids, al-Manṣūr Ḥājjī, began his second reign in 791/1389, the *bayʿa* was given by the caliph and the judges in association, a procedure which was repeated on the accession of al-Ẓāhir Ṭaṭar in 824/1421. This suggests that the caliph was no longer regarded as even nominally the sovereign of the Islamic community, but was assimilated in status to the four chief judges. An even more startling view is implied by Khalīl al-Ẓāhirī, writing in the reign of al-Ẓāhir Jaqmaq (824-57/1438-53), who says that after the Prophet

> 'the caliphate passed to the Imām Abū Bakr al-Ṣiddīq; then the Companions and the caliphs inherited it, one after another until now it has come to be by the *bayʿa* from the Commander of the Faithful, by agreement of the electors, the *ʿulamā'* and the great officials of the august state *(al-dawla al-sharīfa)*, and the consent of their lordships the *amīrs* and the divinely assisted armies.'[1]

This implies that the caliph's *bayʿa* transmitted the caliphate itself to the sultan. Juridically this was extravagant and untenable: historically, it is not surprising that a new doctrine should appear in a time when the caliph was no more than a pensioner at the court of the sultan. The logical conclusion of the development was what in fact happened after the conquest of the Mamluk state by the Ottoman sultan Selīm. The last of the ʿAbbasid caliphs had been captured by Selīm at Marj Dābiq in 922/1516, and thereafter faded quickly out of history. The Ottoman sultan had no need of him as a legitimating authority. It is noteworthy that a tract written in Arabic shortly after the conquest of Egypt to eulogise Selīm's victories expresses very clearly the view at which Khalīl al-Ẓāhirī had hinted, that the sultan is the successor of the caliphs, and particularly of the Patriarchal Caliphs in the golden age of Islam. Selīm is referred to as 'the absolute King of the Age, who rightfully ascends the throne of the caliphate', 'the reviver of the traces of the Patriarchal Caliphs'; he is even explicitly given the unique caliphal title of 'Commander of the Faithful', *(amīr al-mu'minīn)*. Speaking of the flight of the last Mamluk sultan, al-Ashraf Ṭūmān Bāy, who was still at large when this tract was completed, the writer says:

> 'Ṭūmān Bāy and his soldiery fled. Even if the days and times of his flight are prolonged, his power will not equal the power of the caliphate.'[2]

The story, once generally accepted, that Selīm received the caliphate from the last ʿAbbasid has been shown to be an eighteenth-century fabrication: it may nevertheless be reminiscent of a doctrine at the end of the Mamluk period.

The transaction between the caliph and the Mamluk sultan was inserted in a series of older accession-observances which embodied conceptions of the sultanate very different from the classical Islamic theory.[3] These observances partly originated from the traditions of its Ayyubid and Seljukid predecessors. The first Mamluk sultan was installed by the collective decision of *amīrs* and the Baḥriyya, that is to say the army officers and the guard of the Ayyubid sultan al-Ṣāliḥ Ayyūb, who had died in the previous year. The Mamluk sultanate retained this elective character throughout its history, although for a century, from 689/1290 to 792/1390 with three brief periods of usurpation, the throne was occupied by the dynasty founded by the sultan al-Manṣūr Qalāwūn (678-89/1279-90). In fact, after 741/1341 the Qalawunid sultans were almost all puppets of the great *amīrs*, who raised and deposed them. On occasions, especially during the period of the Circassian Mamluk sultanate in the ninth/fifteenth century, a sultan would nominate one of his sons as his heir. These attempts to ensure an hereditary succession were never successful, and within a few months or at most a few years the throne was seized by a usurper. The body of electors was never defined: effectively it consisted of the leading *amīrs* resident in Cairo, often the *amīrs* of a victorious faction. There was thus an unresolved paradox at the centre of the constitution of the Mamluk state: in form a despotic monarchy, it was often in practice a veiled oligarchy of the great *amīrs*.

The election or recognition of a sultan was accompanied by other observances. The new ruler assumed a royal style by which he would henceforth be known: thus, Aybak was entitled 'al-Malik al-Muʿizz', Baybars 'al-Malik al-Ẓāhir' and Qalāwūn 'al-Malik al-Manṣūr'. Such styles had been borne by the subordinate rulers of the Seljukid house and by all Ayyubid princes: during the Mamluk period they were with very few exceptions applied only to the sultan and assumed only on accession. At this time also the sultan received an oath of loyalty from the *amīrs*. This might be of either of two kinds; the *bayʿa*, which signified his recognition as ruler, or a sworn covenant of loyalty to him personally *(ḥilf)*. The latter was sometimes converted into a mutual undertaking between the sultan and the great *amīrs*. The enthronement of the sultan was the act declaratory of his assumption of rulership. In the early sultanate, it was followed by a procession through Cairo.

From the accession of al-Muẓaffar Baybars in 708/1309, the procession was within the precincts of the Citadel to the place of the sultan's enthronement. In this procession, the insignia of the sultanate were displayed: a gilded saddle-cover *(ghāshiya)* - again in imitation of Ayyubid and Seljukid practice - and a parasol surmounted by the figure of a bird in silver-gilt *(al-qubba wa'l-ṭayr)*. The parasol, the trappings of the royal steed, the cloth of the sultan's banners and the livery of his pages were all yellow, the distinctive colour of the regime. The pre-eminence of the sultan was symbolised by the fact that he alone rode while the *amīrs* walked, and at some stage in the proceedings they prostrated themselves before him.

The sultanate had begun in the crisis of 648/1250, when the Mamluks of al-Ṣāliḥ Ayyūb, who had withstood the Crusaders of Louis IX, assassinated the new sultan, al-Muʿaẓẓam Tūrān Shāh, and installed first Shajar al-Durr (the widow of al-Ṣāliḥ Ayyūb) and then one of themselves, al-Muʿizz Aybak, as head of the state. Although Louis IX had been defeated, the Latin kingdom of Jerusalem remained for nearly half a century longer as a potential base for operations against Egypt and Syria. Ten years later the Mamluk sultanate, facing the advance of the apparently invincible Mongol forces of Hülegü, repulsed them at ʿAyn Jālūt in 658/1260, but the realm of the *īl-khāns* in the eastern Fertile Crescent and Persia continued to be for several decades a hostile and infidel neighbour to the Mamluk state. The Mamluk sultan during the first sixty years of the sultanate was therefore primarily a warrior and a leader of warriors, but his military character may be viewed in two rather different ways. Medieval Muslim writers present him in terms of the classic Islamic concept of the fighter in the Holy War *(jihād)* against the unbeliever. In the diploma issued in the name of the caliph al-Mustanṣir to al-Ẓāhir Baybars the sultan is eulogised in these terms:

> 'By thee God has preserved the protection of Islam from decline; by thy resolution the order of these administrations has been maintained. Thy sword has made incurable wounds in the hearts of the unbelievers. There is hope that by thee the seat of the caliphate may be restored to where it was in earlier days. Open for the victory of Islam those eyes which have not slumbered nor slept. In the Holy War against the enemies of God be a leader, not a follower. Support the creed of unity, and in its support you will find only those who hear and obey.'[4]

The same concept was applied to later sultans. Khalīl al-Ẓāhirī, enumerating the honorifics of al-Ẓāhir Jaqmaq, who ruled in the middle of the ninth/fifteenth century when the danger from infidel powers could hardly have been less, entitles the sultan 'the one who cuts off the unbelievers and the polytheists.'[5]

This was, so to speak, the official presentation of the sultan as warrior. But lying behind it was a much more primitive and barbaric concept, of the sultan as a leader of tribal warriors, a *Heerkönig*, whose authority rested on his acceptance by his companions and was buttressed by his personal prowess. Admittedly in Egypt the tribe was synthetic, the Mamluk community consisting of men who had mostly come into Egypt under the form of slavery before being converted to Islam, trained in warfare and emancipated. On the other hand, it seems clear that during the early decades of the sultanate, the Mamluk community was very homogeneous, being mainly recruited from Kipchak Turks. Professor Ayalon has drawn our attention to the anomalous situation of other immigrant warriors, especially the Wāfidiyya Mongols, in this community;[6] and we may note also that when the Circassians came to preponderate they in turn acquired the sultanate. This homogeneity of the Mamluk community contrasts with, for example, the policy of recruitment followed by Maḥmūd of Ghazna.[7]

Besides his military functions, the Mamluk sultan like his Ayyubid predecessors was always and necessarily the mainspring of the administration. His signature was indispensable to validate decrees, even on quite trifling matters as some of the archives of the monastery of St. Catherine on Mount Sinai demonstrate. This at times led to problems. A poignant anecdote is told of al-Ashraf Küchük, a grandson of al-Manṣūr Qalāwūn, who was raised briefly to the sultanate in 742/1341 at no more than seven years of age. When decrees were ready to be signed, his regent would put a pen in his hand, 'and then the teacher came who was teaching him to read the Qur'ān, and he would write the signature with the pen in the hand of al-Ashraf Küchük.'[8] Such a situation was, however, unusual: the sultan normally wrote his own signature, although some sultans may have been barely literate in Arabic.

The sultan exercised his functions as ruler publicly by the holding of his court *(khidma)* in the Citadel. Courts were held for a variety of purposes: the reception of foreign ambassadors, the distribution of *iqṭā'*s after the great cadastral surveys carried out by al-Nāṣir Muḥammad (715-16/1315) as well as routine business. Of this, the most important category was the redress of wrongs through the hearing and answering of petitions. This was central to the sultan's functions as a Muslim ruler, so much so that the building in which the courts were held was known as *dār al-'adl*, the palace of justice. The first *dār al-'adl* in the Citadel was built by al-Ẓāhir Baybars in 661/1262-3, very early in his reign, possibly to emphasise the plenitude of power devolved upon him by the caliph, and following the precedent set by the *atabeg* Nūr al-Dīn Maḥmūd the Zangid.[9] A new hall *(īwān)* for the holding of courts was begun by al-Manṣūr Qalāwūn, completed by his successor, al-Ashraf Khalīl, and rebuilt in more splendid fashion by al-Nāṣir Muḥammad. When the sultanate passed to the Circassians with the accession of al-Ẓāhir Barqūq, the practice of holding court in the *īwān* fell into disuse. A brief formal session took place there, followed by the actual meeting for business in the royal stable.

This change may have been for reasons of security, since the stable, unlike the *īwān*, lay outside the inner residential precinct of the Citadel.

The procedure in the *īwān* during the reign of al-Nāṣir Muḥammad (d. 741/1341) was described by Ibn Faḍlallāh al-ʿUmarī (d. 749/1349) whose account forms the basis of the later descriptions by al-Maqrīzī (d. 845/1442) and Ibn Taghrībirdī (d. 874/1470).[10] The dignitaries took their places according to a strict order of precedence. The positions of greatest honour on the sultan's right hand were allotted to the officers of the religious institution: the four chief judges, the commissioner of *bayt al-māl* (the original Islamic treasury) and the head officer of the *ḥisba* in Cairo, whose function was nominally that of *censor morum*. The precedence of these officials marked the character of the sultanate as an Islamic polity, and bore witness to the survival and prestige of ancient Muslim institutions. An indication of governmental realities was given by the presence of the sultan's secretary *(kātib al-sirr)*, seated on the ruler's left hand. The great office-holders such as the *wazīr* and the vicegerent *(nā'ib al-salṭana)* stood in the sultan's presence. A number of senior *amīrs* of the highest rank sat at a distance from the sultan. They were designated *umarā' al-mashūra*, 'the *amīrs* of the council', but there seems to be no evidence that they constituted a body of councillors to whom the sultan had regular recourse. A group of clerks, known as *kuttāb al-dast*, 'the clerks of the bench', was in attendance.

Al-Nāṣir Muḥammad held court in this fashion every Monday throughout the year except in Ramaḍān. His secretary read the petitions of civilians, and where they raised matters coming under the *Sharīʿa*, the sultan consulted the judges. The petitions of military *iqṭāʿ*-holders were read by the head of the army office *(nāẓir al-jaysh)*. On these, the sultan sought the advice of his chamberlain *(ḥājib)* and the clerk of the army office *(kātib al-jaysh)*. In other matters he acted according to his sole discretion. Another court was held on Thursday. In al-Nāṣir Muḥammad's time, it did not deal with petitions, and the judges, clerks and clerk of the army office were not normally present. Under the later Qalawunids, however, it was expanded into a full court for the hearing of petitions. Al-Ẓāhir Barqūq further increased the time allotted to petitions, which he heard on three days in the week, and this was the current practice when al-Maqrīzī wrote in 819/1416-17. The procedure about this time is briefly described by Ibn Taghrībirdī in his account of the regency of Ṭaṭar, who shortly afterwards usurped the throne:

> 'Then on Friday [20 Muḥarram 824/25 Jan. 1421] proclamation was made that the senior *amīr* Ṭaṭar would sit to judge among the people. So when the prayer was finished, the senior *amīr* Ṭaṭar went and sat in the sessions-hall of the royal stable, as [the sultan] al-Malik al-Mu'ayyad [Shaykh] used to sit in judgement there. He [Ṭaṭar] however sat to the left of the chair

> of state, and did not sit on it. The *amīrs* of the state were in attendance as was customary, and the secretary, the judge Kamāl al-Dīn b. al-Bārizī sat on the platform, and read him the petitions. The adjutant of the army *(naqīb al-jaysh)*, the chief of police of Cairo *(wālī al-Qāhira)* and the chamberlains stood before him. He judged among the subjects, redressed wrongs, and administered excellent justice to the people.'[11]

The justice thus dispensed by the sultan, known as *al-siyāsa*, was in form merely supplementary to the justice administered by the judges in accordance with the *Sharī'a*. It had its antecedents in the *maẓālim* jurisdiction which had developed under the caliphate. In practice it was both more speedy and more effective than the justice of the *Sharī'a* courts, since it derived from the arbitrary will of the sultan, and was enforced by his personal power. It is therefore not surprising that the sultans were increasingly occupied with business of this kind.

The sultan was the supreme but not the only exponent of the *siyāsa*. Before the third reign of al-Nāṣir Muḥammad (709-41/1310-41), the hearing of petitions seems normally to have been delegated to a deputy. Al-Maqrīzī says that al-Mu'izz Aybak appointed Aydikīn al-Bunduqdārī as his vicegerent in Egypt, and he sat with 'the deputies of the palace of justice' *(nuwwāb dār al-'adl)* to hear wrongs.[12] From the reign of al-Ẓāhir Baybars to that of al-Manṣūr Qalāwūn, when the old palace of justice was in use,

> 'always on the days of session, the deputy of the palace of justice *(nā'ib dār al-'adl)* would sit there, and with him the judges, the clerk of the palace of justice and the *amīrs*. The deputy of the palace of justice would investigate the cases of plaintiffs, and the petitions would be read to him.'[13]

These sessions continued when the *īwān* was built, and only after the rebuilding of the *īwān* by al-Nāṣir Muḥammad did it become the regular practice for the sultan himself to hold sessions to hear and determine petitions. Normally, it would seem, the deputy of the palace of justice was none other than the vicegerent of the realm *(nā'ib al-salṭana bi'l-diyār al-Miṣriyya)*. This appears to be the import of a passage which al-Qalqashandī cites from Ibn Faḍlallāh al-'Umarī, written after al-Nāṣir Muḥammad had allowed the office to lapse. The passage mentions the attendance of the vicegerent when the sultan held court in the *īwān*, and then speaks of his adjourning to his own residence *(dār al-niyāba)* with the holders of offices to hold a public session for the hearing of petitions. The writer says expressly that

> 'when the vicegerency was established in this fashion, the sultan did not concern himself personally with the reading of petitions and the hearing of grivances.'[14]

The third reign of al-Nāṣir Muḥammad saw another innovation in the system of royal courts. In 713-4/1314 he built a new palace, al-Qaṣr al-Ablaq, in the Citadel. Here he held court daily, apart from the two days when he sat in the *īwān*. Those who attended were, however, a smaller company and did not usually include the *umarā' al-mashūra* or the senior *amīrs*. When the session ended at the third hour of the day, the sultan retired to his private apartments. Later in the day, he would hold a council on the business of the kingdom in the Inner Palaces (al-Quṣūr al-Juwāniyya) which connected al-Qaṣr al-Ablaq with his private apartments. To this council the sultan would summon those office-holders whom he required, such as the *wazīr*, the secretary, the controller of the privy purse and the head of the army office. The accounts of al-Maqrīzī and al-Qalqashandī thus suggest that in this reign the sultan presided over four types of assembly of dignitaries, ranging from public and extremely formal court for hearing petitions *(khidmat al-Īwān)* to the small council of officials on state affairs *(khidmat al-Qaṣr)*.[15] The proliferation of these assemblies in the third reign of al-Nāṣir Muḥammad, the suspension of the vicegerent's office, and the inauguration of the personal hearing of petitions by the same sultan reflect a change in the circumstances of the monarchy. Earlier sultans had been preoccupied by the danger from the Mongols and campaigns against the Frankish states. Al-Nāṣir Muḥammad was the first sultan who did not need to make an expedition almost annually to Syria. During most of his third reign Damascus was committed to his great viceroy, the *amīr* Tankiz al-Nāṣirī, and the Mamluk sultanate entered on a peaceful period which lasted almost until the end of the century.

The usage in the time of the sultan al-Ẓāhir Jaqmaq (842-57/1438-53) is described by Khalīl al-Ẓāhirī.[16] At this time the *īwān* was used only for the reception of important ambassadors. Ordinary courts were held twice a week: on Mondays and Thursdays in al-Qaṣr al-Ablaq, and (at the end of winter and beginning of spring) in the royal stable. The full proceedings consisted of four parts: first, a review of troops; secondly, the approval and signature by the sultan of grants of *iqṭā'*s and other decrees; thirdly, a session to give judgements; finally, a state banquet.

The sultan was served by three categories of officials, who are designated in the sources 'the Men of the Sword' *(arbāb al-suyūf)*, 'the Men of the Pen' *(arbāb al-qalam)*, and 'the Men of the Religious Establishment' *(arbāb al-waẓā'if al-dīniyya)*. The first of these categories formed a military aristocracy, chiefly composed of Mamluks who had been recruited directly from their homelands, then trained, emancipated and promoted to amirates. The *amīrs* were not only the commanders of the armed forces but also the holders of the great household and administrative offices. The sons and later descendants of Mamluks, known as *awlād al-nās* 'the sons of the people', did not usually obtain similar preferment because the political structure of the sultanate was inimical to their advancement. There are, however, numerous exceptions to this general rule: the chroniclers frequently mention an *amīr* who was the son of an *amīr*. Instances of this are perhaps commonest under the later Qalawunids. One sultan of this period, al-Nāṣir Ḥasan (748-52/1347-51, 755-62/1354-61), made it his policy to promote *awlād al-nās* to the superior amirates and high office. This was exceptional: for the most part such men had to be content with the subordinate rank of *amīr* of Ten. The military institution as a whole comprised in addition the Royal Mamluks *(al-mamālīk al-sulṭāniyya)*, the troopers of the *Ḥalqa* (originally the bodyguard of the Ayyubid ruler but under the Mamluks an obsolescent military formation), and the Mamluk retainers of the *amīrs*. The military institution was maintained from concessions (sing. *iqṭa*ʻ), formally of the land-tax of specific villages practically of the villages themselves. Al-Qalqashandi described the *iqṭā*ʻ*s* in these words:

> 'The *iqṭā*ʻ*s* in this kingdom are granted to the *amīrs* and the troopers. Generally the *iqṭā*ʻ*s* are villages and lands, of which the holder *(muqṭa*ʻ*)* has the usufruct and which he may manage as he will. Sometimes they include money which he receives from sources of revenue, and this is uncommon.'[17]

Elsewhere[18] he mentions that most of the best land in Egypt was held by the *amīrs*, a single *iqṭā*ʻ consisting of one to ten villages. Second-class land was held by the Royal Mamluks, two or more usually sharing a village. Land of the lowest class was held by the troopers of the *ḥalqa*, a number of whom shared a single village. Arab tribesmen who had duties concerning the routes and mail-service ranked as *iqṭā*ʻ-holders of this third class. Unlike the military aristocracy, the Men of the Pen and of the Religious Establishment (two categories which overlapped in practice) were natives of Egypt and Syria, together with some free-born Muslim immigrants. The Men of the Pen, however, normally included *dhimmīs* (i.e. Christians, Jews and Samaritans) as well as converts to Islam.

A useful starting point for investigating the great offices of the Mamluk sultanate is provided by al-Qalqashandī's chapter on the Officers of the Presence *(man huwa bi-ḥaḍrat al-sulṭān)*.[19] His data must, however, be used with some caution, since his encyclopaedic work, *Ṣubḥ al-a*ʻ*shā*, conflates material concerning practices current in his own time and information derived from earlier writers. *Ṣubḥ al-a*ʻ*shā* was completed in 812/1412, that is, early in the Circassian Mamluk sultanate, but in this chapter as elsewhere, al-Qalqashandī quotes extensively from Ibn Faḍlallāh al-ʻUmarī, who served as a chancery official under al-Nāṣir Muḥammad and died in 749/1349. Between the time of al-Umarī and that of al-Qalqashandī the evolution of offices had not stood still, and it is not always easy to be certain that al-Qalqashandī is describing the situation as it existed in his own time. In addition, both men were civil servants, and a comparison of their accounts with data afforded by the chroniclers suggests that at times their presentation is over-systematic - a description of administration as it ought to have been rather than as it was.

Al-Qalqashandī lists in this chapter twenty-five offices, arranged approximately in order of their importance, but not classified in any way. However, it is clear that only two or three of them are, strictly speaking, public offices: those namely of the vicegerent *(nā'ib al-salṭana)*, with which may be reckoned that of the acting vicegerent *(nā'ib al-ghayba)*, the *atābak*, and the chiefs of police in the capital and the Citadel. All the others were in form, and very largely in function, offices of the royal household, although a distinction may be made between those offices of which the holders served the sultan in his public or ceremonial capacity, and the domestic offices properly speaking. These last may be quickly dismissed, since al-Qalqashandī lists only two: the office of the commander of the Mamluks *(taqaddumat al-Mamālīk)*, who was responsible for the Royal Mamluks in training, and that of the comptroller of the royal apartments *(zimāmiyyat al-dūr al-sulṭāniyya)*. Significantly, both these domestic offices were held by black eunuchs, who were, however, incorporated in the Mamluk system of rank with the grade of *amīr ṭablkhānāh*, i.e. an *amīr* of the second grade.

The two offices which head al-Qalqashandī's list are those of the vicegerent and the *atābak*. With regard to the first, we should note that the main element in his title, *nā'ib*, was used for officers of very different ranks and functions, including the governors of the Syrian provinces and the castellans of the royal fortresses. The vicegerent was, however, distinguished by being styled *al-nā'ib al-kāfil* and *kāfil al-mamālik al-Islāmiyya*, i.e. the vicegerent of the Empire. The term *kāfil* was not quite exclusive to the vicegerent; it was also applied to the *nā'ib* of Damascus, who as the sultan's representative in an ancient capital had the status of a viceroy rather than of an ordinary provincial governor. The association of sovereignty with Damascus was a recurrent and troublesome theme throughout and even after the Mamluk sultanate. From Sanjar al-Ḥalabī in 658/1260 to Jānbardī al-Ghazālī in 926/1520, after the Ottoman conquest, a number of governors of Damascus assumed royal titles and sought to establish their independence.

By the chroniclers, the vicegerent is usually styled *nā'ib al-salṭana bi'l-diyār al-Miṣriyya*, 'the deputy of the sultanate in Egypt'. His functions as described by al-ʿUmarī (cited by al-Qalqashandī) were very extensive indeed, and amounted to a plenary delegation of the sultan's powers in administration and jurisdiction. In al-ʿUmarī's words, 'He is within limits a sultan - indeed he is the second sultan.' Nevertheless, although he was drawn from the Men of the Sword and was an *amīr* of the highest rank, he did not hold any military command. The lapse of the vicegerency during the third reign of al-Nāṣir Muḥammad was a development fully in keeping with that sultan's autocratic style as a ruler. Although a vicegerent was again appointed after his death, and the series continued, not without interruptions, until 810/1407-8, the office never regained its former pre-eminence. This decline of the vicegerency is connected with the development of two other offices, that of chamberlain *(ḥajib)*, and that of the *atābak*.

The title of *atābak al-ʻasākir* is rendered by Popper 'commander-in-chief of the armies'. Popper goes on to say, with reference to the Circassian Mamluk sultanate, that this officer 'had no duties except those of leading the armies in action and, generally, sitting on the Sultan's advisory council'.[20] Ayalon states that 'he was commander-in-chief of the army, but his functions were much broader, as indicated by the frequently appended title of *mudabbir al-mamālik* or *mudabbir al-mamālik al-islāmiyya*.'[21] These definitions are over-simplifications of a long and complex development, and two matters need to be distinguished. The first is that of the nature and evolution of the office of *atābak*, the second that of the relationship between the *atābakiyya* and the *tadbīr al-mamlaka*. The term *atābak* itself is the arabicised form of the Turkish *atabeg*, which was used under the Great Seljuk sultans to signify a military officer (hence, usually, a Mamluk) who was the protector of a young Seljukid prince. As is well known, on the fragmentation of the Seljuk empire, power in various regions was usurped by *atabegs*, who themselves founded dynasties. Through its Ayyubid predecessor, the Mamluk sultanate was linked with one of these, the dynasty established in Syria by the *atabeg* Zangī.

In Mamluk Egypt, the usual designation was *atābak al-ʻasākir*, although there are a number of variants: *muqaddam al-ʻaskar*, *atābak al-juyūsh*, and so forth. In itself, *atābak al-ʻasākir* indicated an officer who was authorised to exercise the chief military command in place of the sultan. Thus, just before the Mamluk usurpation of the sultanate, when al-Ṣāliḥ Ayyūb died in 647/1249, his son and heir al-Muʻaẓẓam Tūrān Shāh being absent from Egypt, the *amīr* Fakhr al-Dīn Yūsuf b. Shaykh al-Shuyūkh was appointed *atābak al-ʻasākir*. Here the command was being exercised on behalf of a dead or absent ruler. When in the following year al-Muʻaẓẓam Tūrān Shāh was murdered, and Shajar al-Durr was proclaimed queen, the appointment of an *atābak* to hold the chief command on her behalf was necessary. The *amīr* Aybak, who was then appointed, married the queen and usurped the sultanate. Under pressure however, he had to agree to the installation of an Ayyubid child, al-Ashraf Mūsā, as nominal sultan, and Aybak reverted to the status of *atābak* until he was able to repeat his usurpation. The *atābak* exercising command in military affairs on behalf of a minor became a regular feature of the sultanate, examples being the *atābaks* of al-Manṣūr ʻAlī b. Aybak, of al-ʻĀdil Salāmish, and of al-Nāṣir Muḥammad b. Qalāwūn. The *atābak* of al-ʻĀdil Salāmish was Qalāwūn the usurper.

After the death of al-Nāṣir Muḥammad in 741/1341, the office of *atābak* did not immediately reappear, although several of his successors were very young. The powerful *amīrs* who acted as regents for the first four of these later Qalawunids bore the title of *mudabbir al-mamlaka* (or a variant of this) signifying 'the administrator of the kingdom'. Some, but not all, of the earlier *atābaks*, including Fakhr al-Dīn Yūsuf b. Shaykh al-Shuyūkh, had also been *mudabbirs*, but the two titles could be separately held and were not synonymous: whereas the *atābakiyya* was a delegation of the supreme military command, *tadbīr* was executive power in the administration. *Mudabbir* had, indeed, been a title of the Mamluk *wazīr*, and is so mentioned by al-Qalqashandī.[22] In the time of the later Qalawunids, when the Mamluk sultanate was mainly at peace in external affairs, there was little need for an *atābak* of the old style, although there was much scope for a regent acting in the name of a shadow-sultan. Under the last Qalawunids the two titles of *atābak* and *mudabbir* were successively held together by several of the more powerful and ambitious *amīrs*, and finally by Barqūq, who ended by usurping the throne of his nominal sultan, and thereby inaugurated the Circassian Mamluk succession.

There are two other innovations concerning the *atābakiyya* in the late Qalawunid period. The *atābak* Shaykhūn in the reign of al-Nāṣir Ḥasan (756/1355-6) assumed the title of *al-amīr al-kabīr*, 'the senior *amīr*'. Commenting on this, Ibn Taghrībirdī remarks as follows:

> 'He was the first *atābak* to be called *al-amīr al-kabīr*, and after him to our own day the *atābakiyya* has become an office with investiture by a robe. But in those days, an *amīr* who had priority in immigration was called *al-amīr al-kabīr* without any investiture, so that at any one time there would be a company, every one of whom was called *al-amīr al-kabīr*; until, when Shaykhūn exercised the office of *atābak al-ʻasākir* and was called *al-amīr al-kabīr*, that old custom lapsed, and it became one of the most exalted offices of the *amīrs*.'[23]

In other words, the *atābakiyya* ceased to be an *ad hoc* appointment, and, having lost its original specifically military significance, it became synonymous with primacy among the *amīrs*. It did not necessarily even imply a regency. At the very end of the Mamluk sultanate Ibn Iyās, listing the dignitaries at the beginning of the year 922/1516, mentions after the caliph, the sultan and the four chief judges 'the *atābakī* Sūdūn min Jānī Bak al-ʻAjamī *amīr kabīr*.'[24] The sultan was the octogenarian al-Ashraf Qānṣawh al-Ghawrī, who a few months later was to lead his army in battle against the Ottomans. Clearly, Sūdūn was neither regent nor commander-in-chief, he was just the senior *amīr*.

The second innovation concerning the *atābakiyya* in the late Qalawunid period was the proliferation of this office, or rather of this rank. Beginning, so far as I know, with the *amīr* Mankalībughā al-Shamsī in 769/1367, there appears the new style of *atābak al-ʻasākir bi'l-diyār al-Miṣriyya*, i.e. *atābak* in Egypt, while about twenty years later we start to read of *atābaks* of Aleppo and Damascus. This seems to confirm the development of the *atābakiyya* from an office with specific functions to a rank indicating precedence.

By a development analogous to that which took place at the courts of medieval Europe, several of the household offices of the Mamluk sultanate acquired public functions - an evolution which was noted by some chroniclers. One of these was the office of the *dawādār*, whose original duty (as the term suggests) was to carry the royal inkwell when the sultan affixed his sign-manual to documents. At first this had been a minor post, held by a civilian. In the reign of al-Ẓāhir Baybars it, like other offices listed by Ibn Taghrībirdī, was militarized, but was held only by a low-ranking *amīr* of Ten. But under the late Qalawunids, the *dawādāriyya* was occupied by an *amīr* of the highest rank; it had spawned a staff of subordinates (the head by then being styled *dawādār kabīr*), and it served as the connecting link between the sultan and the civilian secretarial body. By the end of the Mamluk sultanate, the *dawādār kabīr* may not inappropriately be styled the secretary of state. Under al-Ashraf Qānṣawh al-Ghawrī, the post was held by Ṭūmān Bāy, a relative of the sultan and his successor after the catastrophe of Marj Dābiq.

Another office which was militarized, rose in status and extended its functions was that of the chamberlain *(ḥājib)* who, from being a mere doorkeeper, became a great officer with judicial functions. Like the *dawādāriyya*, the *ḥujūbiyya* evolved into a plurality of offices, headed by the great chamberlain *(ḥājib al-ḥujjāb)*, an *amīr* of the highest rank. A similar development may be traced in what was originally a household office *par excellence*, that of the high steward *(ustādār)*, whose responsibility was at the start for the royal kitchen and buttery, and their staff. Although the *ustādār* never attained the dominating position of a Merovingian mayor of the palace, he acquired, as we shall see, considerable financial powers. Like the great chamberlain, the high steward was an *amīr* of the highest rank and had a staff of subordinates.

Besides these great offices at the sultan's court and in the capital of the empire, the Men of the Sword also held the provincial governorships in Syria. First of these in precedence was the governorship of Damascus *(niyābat al-Shām)*, then that of Aleppo, the northern capital, followed by Tripoli and the smaller provinces of Ḥamāh, Ṣafad and al-Karak. At the beginning of the Mamluk period, of course, these Syrian territories had not formed part of the sultan's dominions but were under Ayyubid or Frankish rule. The Mongol invasion of 657-8/1259-60 broke the power of the Ayyubids, leaving the pieces to be picked up by al-Ẓāhir Baybars after ʿAyn Jālūt. The Ayyubid principality of Ḥamāh survived under Mamluk suzerainty until 698/1299, and was restored (in the person of the scholar and chronicler Abu'l-Fidā') in 710/1310. It was finally brought under direct rule in 742/1341. Other territories, which lay on the fringe of the empire were ruled by local dynasties under the domination but not the detailed control of the sultan. This was the situation of the Christian neighbours of the sultanate: Lesser Armenia, the Frankish states of Antioch-Tripoli and the Latin kingdom and in the far south the Nubian kingdom of al-Muqurra. In course of time, these protectorates ceased to exist. The last remnants of Frankish territory were absorbed into Mamluk Syria after al-Ashraf Khalīl's campaign in 690/1291. Lesser Armenia, long a prey to Mamluk raids, was finally extinguished in 776/1375, and on its former territory the Turcoman dynasty of Banū Ramaḍān (Ramazanoğulları) established itself at Adana in virtual independence of the Mamluk sultanate. To the west and the east lay two other Turcoman dynastic lands: Karaman, established in the second half of the seventh/thirteenth century, and Elbistan, ruled from 738/1337 by the Dulghādir clan. As regards al-Muqurra, a campaign in 716/1316 placed a Nubian prince converted to Islam on the throne. During the later part of the century, al-Muqurra ceased to exist as a unified kingdom.

The Men of the Pen staffed an elaborate and highly organised civil service, of which the antecedents in Egypt went back to the Fatimid caliphate, and which in the Mamluk period extended its competence over Syria as well, although the provincial governors there had their own civil services for local purposes. There were three main divisions of the administrative organisation: the chancery *(dīwān al-inshā')*, the army office *(dīwān al-jaysh)*, and the fiscal departments. In the past, the chief minister had borne the title of *wazīr* and had exercised plenary powers. The title survived under the Mamluk sultanate, and Khalīl al-Ẓāhirī's discussion of the office suggests that even in the mid-ninth/fifteenth century it retained a primacy of esteem. In fact, however, the sultan's chief minister had long been the head of the chancery *(nāẓir dīwān al-inshā', ṣāḥib dīwān al-inshā')*, who had emerged from among his brother-clerks during the reign of al-Manṣūr Qalāwūn and was distinguished as the secretary *(kātib al-sirr)*. The first to hold this office and title was the *qāḍī* Fatḥ al-Dīn b. Muḥyī al-Dīn b. ʿAbd al-Ẓāhir. He, like his successors, was an Islamic scholar by training, but his functions as secretary were quite distinct from those of a *qāḍī*. There was a tendency to secretarial dynasticism: the father of Fatḥ al-Dīn had been one of a triumvirate of chief clerks who had preceded the inauguration of the sole secretaryship. Subsequently, members of four generations of Banū Faḍlallāh held the secretaryship at various dates between 692/1293 and 796/1394.[25] Besides his duties as a departmental head, the secretary was in frequent and close attendance on the sultan, reading the incoming despatches and serving generally as adviser. His chancery was staffed by two classes of clerks: a superior order, known as the clerks of the bench *(kuttāb al-dast)*, who had originally been the equals of the secretary, and continued to attend the sultan's court with him; and an inferior order, the clerks of the roll *(kuttāb al-darj)* who were employed in the writing-office. There were strict rules for the minuting and dating of state papers, and a regular procedure controlled the passage of documents originating in the chancery and other departments, or as petitions, to the authorisation of appropriate action.

An important class of business originated in the army office, which was not a war department but was primarily concerned with grants of *iqṭāʿ* to Men of the Sword. Here the procedure might be started in one of three different ways: by an order from the head of the army office *(nāẓir dīwān al-jaysh)*, by private petition, or by a certificate of relinquishment. After due authorisation, a warrant *(murabbaʿa)* for the grant of an *iqṭāʿ* was drawn up by a clerk in the army office and passed to the chancery, where a patent *(manshūr)* was engrossed.

This was validated by the sultan's signature - an act which, it seems, regularly took place in open court.

The original state treasury of the Mamluk sultanate was in the charge of the *wazīr*, and hence was known as *dīwān al-wizāra*, 'the office of the wazirate'. A synonym was *al-dawla al-sharīfa*, 'the august treasury'. These fiscal functions were all that remained to the once omnicompetent *wazīr*, who was usually one of the Men of the Pen, but might be chosen from the military aristocracy. A vestige of a still more ancient institution, *bayt al-māl*, the name of the original Islamic treasury, survived as a sub-department of *dīwān al-wizāra*, and administered certain specific revenues such as inheritance dues *(al-mawārīth al-ḥashriyya)*. A second treasury, the sultan's privy purse *(dīwān al-khāṣṣ, d. al-khawāṣṣ)*, received the revenues accruing from the crown estates as well as income from other sources. The importance of the privy purse increased in the third reign of al-Nāṣir Muḥammad. The great cadastral survey and redistribution of *iqṭā'*s which he carried out in 715/1315-16 increased the crown estates from one-sixth to five-twelfths of the taxable land of Egypt. When he abolished the wazirate, the head of the privy purse department *(nāẓir dīwān al-khāṣṣ)* became for a time the principal fiscal official. Al-Ẓāhir Barqūq established a new household treasury, *al-dīwān al-mufrad*, originally to handle the *iqṭā'*s which had been held by his eldest son, Nāṣir al-Dīn Muḥammad, who died in 797/1395. These revenues were expended on the Royal Mamluks and the domestic officers of the palace. The department was headed by the high steward *(ustādār)* and was alternatively known as *dīwān al-ustādāriyya*. As a member of the military aristocracy, the high steward enjoyed greater prestige than the head of the privy purse, who was a Man of the Pen. *Al-dīwān al-mufrad* continued to exist under later sultans, as also did another household treasury established by al-Ẓāhir Barqūq, viz. *dīwān al-amlāk*, which administered the revenue arising from the properties of the sultan. This personal treasury was also under the high steward.

The Men of the Religious Establishment comprised the holders of a variety of offices ranging from the chief judges *(qāḍī al-quḍāt)* to the teachers of the religious sciences. In practice, as we have seen, the caliph was associated with this category at the institution of a new sultan, but significantly he was not present when the sultan held court in *dār al-'adl* and formal precedence was given to the religious office-holders. Of these, the four chief judges occupied the highest rank. In the earliest years of the Mamluk sultanate, as under previous regimes, there had been a single chief judge in Egypt. The appointment of four chief judges, one for each of the Sunnī law-schools (sing. *madhhab*) which were authoritative in the sultan's dominions, was first made by al-Ẓāhir Baybars in 663/1265, ostensibly in order to expedite judicial business. Personal rancour between the sultan's adviser, the *amīr* Aydughdī al-'Azīzī, and the chief judge Tāj al-Dīn 'Abd al-Wahhāb b. Bint al-A'azz, was, however, a motive at work behind the reform. Thereafter four chief judges held office concurrently until the Ottoman conquest. Although these men and their deputies (sing. *nā'ib*) administered justice in the *Sharī'a* courts, their jurisdiction was in practice largely restricted to civil cases between ordinary Muslims. As a consequence of the historic development of the Holy Law of Islam, only certain specific types of criminal actions came before the *qāḍī*'s court, and criminal justice in general was dispensed by administrative officers. In Mamluk Egypt the heads of this system were the two (sometimes three) chiefs of police (sing. *wālī*) for the cities of Cairo and al-Fusṭāṭ, and their two colleagues in the Citadel. Perhaps the only one of whose methods we are told any details is Dawlāt Khujā al-Ẓāhirī, 'a low fellow of Turkish extraction', whom al-Ashraf Barsbāy appointed *wālī* of Cairo in 835/1432, and of whom Ibn Taghrībirdī writes thus:

> 'When he was appointed as *wālī* of Cairo, he began by releasing all the criminals from prison, and he swore to cut in two any of them that he caught thieving. He aroused great terror. He used to ride at night patrolling in absolute security. He kept his oath about the thieves; if one of those whom he had released (he had a note of their names) fell into his hands, he cut him in two. The evil-doers were terrified of him, and gave up thieving. Then he began to tighten up on people and enforced various requirements; e.g. he ordered them to sweep the streets and sprinkle them with water, and every shopkeeper to hang a lantern on his shop, and he punished folk for that. Then he forbade women to go out to the graveyard on Fridays, and many things until people loathed him.'[26]

Justice was also dispensed, as we have seen, by the sultan or his delegate in court on the petitions submitted to him. A growing share in the handling of this kind of judicial business, the *siyāsa* jurisdiction, was taken by the great chamberlain. Originally his competence appears to have been limited to cases arising among the Mamluks, but by the time that al-Maqrīzī wrote in the first half of the ninth/fifteenth century his jurisdiction was encroaching on that of the *Sharī'a* judges.[27]

In conclusion, the Mamluk sultanate was a complex political and social organisation. It had inherent sources of weakness - inevitably clearer to later generations than to contemporaries - but it was a remarkably durable structure with a greater and more effective concentration of military and political power than had existed, except briefly and occasionally, under the Ayyubids. It was, furthermore, not static but a changing and developing polity. The two centuries and a half of the sultanate may be analysed into several periods which differ in their character and in which different historical forces are at work; and evolution of the institutions and offices of the sultanate may also be discerned. We have to do, not with 'a *Colluvies* of slaves' (as Humphrey Prideaux called it)[28] but with a wealthy and sophisticated medieval monarchy, in the extent of its power and perhaps in some features of its governmental structure a worthy predecessor of the Ottoman sultanate which finally overthrew it.

P. M. HOLT

1. Khalīl b. Shāhīn al-Ẓāhirī, *Kitāb zubdat kashf al-mamālik wa-bayān al-ṭuruq wa'l-masālik* (ed. Paul Ravaisse), Paris, 1894, 54.

2. ʻAlī b. Muḥammad al-Lakhmī al-Ishbīlī, *al-Durr al-musān fī sīrat al-muẓaffar Salīm Khān* (ed. Hans Ernst), [n. p.], 1962, 2, 3, 6, 13.

3. A fuller study of these and related matters is included in my article, 'The position and power of the Mamluk sultan', *BSOAS*, XXXVIII, 1975, 237-49.

4. S. F. Sadeque, *Baybars the First of Egypt*, Dacca, 1956; my own translation from p.41 of the Arabic text of Ibn Abd al-Ẓāhir, *al-Rawḍ al-zāhir fī sīrat al-Malik al-Ẓāhir*.

5. Khalīl al-Ẓāhirī, *Zubdat kashf al-mamālik*, 67.

6. Cf. David Ayalon, 'The Wafidiya in the Mamluk kingdom', *Islamic Culture*, XXV, 1951, 89-104.

7. Cf. C. E. Bosworth, *The Ghaznavids*, 2nd edn., Beirut, 1973, 107-8.

8. Abu'l-Maḥāsin Yūsuf b. Taghrībirdī, *al-Nujūm al-zāhira fī mulūk Miṣr wa'l-Qāhira*. X, [Cairo, n.d.], 49.

9. 'Il convient de noter que Nūr ad-Dīn n'institua le *dār al-ʻadl* à Alep et à Damas que le jour où il reçut du calife les pleins pouvoirs en Syrie, cette haute cour soulignait en fait son rôle de souverain.' Nikita Elisséef, *Nūr ad-Dīn*, Damascus, 1967, 845.

10. The passage from Ibn Faḍlallāh al-ʻUmari is translated in [M.] Gaudefroy-Demombynes, *La Syrie à l'époque des mamelouks*, Paris, 1923, xcviii-c.

11. Ibn Taghrībirdī, *Nujūm*, xiv, 173.

12. Aḥmad b. ʻAlī al-Maqrīzī, *Kitāb al-mawā'iẓ wa'l-iʻtibār bi-dhikr al-khiṭaṭ wa'l-āthār*, Beirut, [n.d.], II, 208.

13. Al-Maqrīzī, *Khiṭat*, II, 206.

14. Aḥmad b. ʻAlī al-Qalqashandī, *Ṣubḥ al-aʻshā fī ṣināʻat al-inshā*, [Cairo, n.d.], IV, 17. The view which I have here expressed differs from that of S. M. Stern, 'Petitions from the Mamlūk period', *BSOAS*, XXIX, 1966, 269.

15. Al-Maqrīzī, *Khiṭaṭ*, II, 208-10; al-Qalqashandī, *Ṣubḥ*, IV, 44-5.

16. Khalīl al-Ẓāhirī, *Zubdat kashf al-mamālik*, 86-7.

17. Al-Qalqashandī, *Ṣubḥ*, IV, 50-1.

18. *Ṣubḥ*, III, 453-4.

19. Al-Qalqashandī, *Ṣubḥ*, IV, 16-23. The substance of this chapter is given in Gaudefroy-Demombynes, *La Syrie*, LV-LXIV.

20. William Popper, *Egypt and Syria under the Circassian sultans 1382-1468 A.D.*, Berkeley and Los Angeles, 1955, 91.

21. David Ayalon, 'Studies on the structure of the Mamluk army', III, *BSOAS*, IXII, 1955, 58; cf. idem, ATABAK AL-ʻASAKIR, *Encyclopaedia of Islam* (2nd. edn.), I, 732.

22. Al-Qalqashandī, *Ṣubḥ*, VI, 264.

23. Ibn Taghrībirdī, *Nujūm*, X, 303.

24. Muḥammad b. Aḥmad b. Iyās, *Badāʼiʻ al-zuhūr fī waqāʼi al-duhūr*, V, (2nd. edn. ed. Mohamad Mostafa), Cairo, 1961, 3.

25. See K. S. Salibi, FAḌL ALLĀH, *Encyclopaedia of Islam* (2nd. edn.), II, 732-3; G. Wiet, 'Les secretaires de la chancellerie (Kuttāb-el-Sirr) en Égypte sous les Mamlouks circassiens (784-922/1382-1517)', *Mélanges René Basset*, Paris, 1923-25, I, 271-314.

26. Ibn Taghrībirdī, *Nūjūm*, XIV, 360.

27. See David Ayalon, 'The great Yāsa of Chingiz Khān, a re-examination' (C2), *Studia Islamica*, XXXVIII, 1973, 107-56; Émile Tyan, *Histoire de l'organisation judiciaire en pays d'Islam*, 2nd. edn., Leiden, 1960, 540-4.

28. Anon., *The life of the Reverend Humphrey Prideaux, D.D., Dean of Norwich*, London, 1748, 268.

Iqṭāʿ and the end of the Crusader states

'For their services, and in proportion to their grades, the [Mamluk] emirs were rewarded with fiefs (Arabic singular *iqṭāʿ*) which might be landed estates (compact or scattered), towns, villages or even annual allowances from the revenue of a tax, customs duty or excise levied by the central government. Each emir was obliged to divide two-thirds of his fief among his own private mamluks, by granting them either portions of the fief, or pecuniary allowances from its revenue.'[1]

M. M. Ziada's description of *iqṭāʿ* is based fairly closely on that given in A. N. Poliak's *Feudalism in Egypt, Syria, Palestine and the Lebanon 1250-1900*,[2] the first work of any substance to focus on the question of the Muslim 'fief', clearly a topic of enormous interest for historians of the Crusader states. Ziada, however, goes on to distinguish between the Western fief and the *iqṭāʿ* on the grounds that as far as the latter was concerned, even where the grant appears to be of a designated area of land, it was not an alienation of property by the state, but rather of the tax revenue leviable on that land. Ziada's description of this form of land tenure assigned to the military classes in medieval Egypt and Syria does not differ significantly from those given by other scholars such as Claude Cahen[3] and Hassanein Rabie.[4]

As a characterisation of an institution which existed throughout the period of the Mamluk regime in Egypt and Syria (roughly 1250-1517) it is lucid and broadly satisfactory. Yet naturally this kind of thumb-nail characterisation of a complex institution over a long period of time conceals more questions than it answers - questions which will come easily to the mind of any student of Western feudal tenure or of the Byzantine institution of *pronoia*. A detailed comparison of Ayyubid or Mamluk *iqṭāʿ* tenure in Syria with Latin fief tenure in the neighbouring Crusader states in the thirteenth century presents itself to the historian as an attractive possibility, but the clarification of a large number of unresolved problems and a much closer examination of *iqṭāʿ* as it evolved in a particular period and place are necessary preconditions for this.

Was the tenure of *iqṭāʿ* restricted to those holding the rank of *amīr* (or 'knights' as A. N. Poliak called them)? What was the comparative extent and importance of *iqṭāʿ* held by Mamluk *amīrs* and non-Mamluk *amīrs*? If we were to grant that *iqṭāʿ* was usually an allocation of tax revenue on a designated area of land to the *muqṭaʿ* (the holder of an *iqṭāʿ*), of which taxes exactly was it a question? And were other sorts of so-to-speak seigneurial revenue being collected on the same area of land by another type of landlord? Was one expected or indeed allowed to reside on one's *iqṭāʿ*? How much military service was owed to the state by the *muqṭaʿ* in any one year? How did the *amīr* raise and maintain the levy he brought with him on campaign? Were particular *iqṭāʿs* tied to the office or the individual? What rights did the provincial governors have to intervene in *iqṭāʿs* within their provinces? How was the value of *iqṭāʿs* calculated and how were they assigned in a period when there were no major cadastral surveys (s. *rawk*)? Did the *muqṭaʿ* collect his revenues in money or in kind? How large an area of the Mamluk sultanate was placed under *iqṭāʿ* compared with other forms of tenure? Given that Mamluk *amīrs* were receiving payment on the eve of campaigns and other occasional largesse on the lavish scale that Ayalon's famous study suggests,[5] what need was there for *iqṭāʿ* at all? A middle-rank *amīr* of forty would receive as *nafaqa* (pay) between four hundred and a thousand dinars, admittedly on an irregular basis, but Professor Ashtor has estimated that a working man could keep himself on an annual income of twelve to eighteen dinars.[6] And do thirteenth-century sources, for instance, use the term *iqṭāʿ* in a sufficiently precise sense for it to bear the sort of weight these questions put upon it?

This paper is concerned with *iqṭāʿ* in Palestine and Syria in the late thirteenth century, using insofar as is possible source material that seems to refer to that time and that place, therefore avoiding as much as possible a synthetic and essentially unhistorical perspective on this important institution. One inevitable result of this approach will be that one is using a much smaller volume of literature, in the form of biographies or chronicles, which is interested in sultans, *ʿulamāʾ* and battles and barely if at all, in institutional history. Insofar as is possible the later encyclopaedias produced by the Mamluk chancery are excluded.

In the context of Syria and Palestine in the late thirteenth century further questions arise in relation to *iqṭāʿ* which are extremely difficult and in many cases impossible to answer. Were there substantial differences between Syrian and Egyptian *iqṭāʿs* and between Syrian and Egyptian *amīrs*? How far had any system of *iqṭāʿ* tenure been worked out and codified in the formative period of the Mamluk state? Will not the *ḥalqa* have been playing a much more important role in this period? And indeed, what exactly was the *ḥalqa*? As the Mamluks came to occupy or in many cases to partition the old Crusader territories and place them under *muqṭaʿs* did the method of levying revenue and the type of revenue levied change?

It is necessary to emphasise the particular significance of Syria and Palestine in the late thirteenth century. As far as the

the period c. 1250-1300 is concerned, it is a time in which the Mamluk system of government is only slowly being worked out. It cannot have sprung up fully grown and equipped like Athene from Zeus's forehead. It is in this period that some traditional offices of government like the *atābak* and the *wazīr* are declining in authority and respect and others such as the *dawādār* and the *ḥājib* are extending their authority. More important for our purposes, it is a period when the 'dynasty' and the 'system' are unstable and loyalty must be paid for rather generously. It is also a period when a lot of newly-acquired lands are coming into the hands of the sultan of Egypt, from the Crusaders and the Kurdish princelings of Syria. The land thereby acquired may be distributed to supporters of the regime, but given the unsettled situation in the area at that time (a product *inter alia* of Latin raiding, the Mongol invasions and of the Syrian revolts) there is no guarantee that lands distributed in *iqṭā‘* will show a certain profit in any year. The Mamluk army was certainly well equipped to take lands from the Crusaders but it was a different matter to ensure their security and prosperity.

Moreover, throughout this period (although we lack detailed and systematic evidence on this subject) it seems clear that the most important Mamluk *iqṭā‘s* were in Syria and Palestine. Certainly there are many more references to them in the sources than there are to Egyptian *iqṭā‘s*. One point of some interest is that in the two crucial preliminary decades before the accession of the sultan Baybars in 1260, Baḥrī Mamluk *iqṭā‘s* were concentrated in Palestine. Plausibly this was an accident of chronology, though a revealing one. The Baḥrī Mamluk regiment was formed by al-Ṣāliḥ Ayyūb of Egypt in the years between 1240 and 1249, precisely at the time when lands were being retaken from the Franks of Palestine. Jerusalem was acquired by al-Ṣāliḥ in 642/1244-5 and its lands handed over in *iqṭā‘* to the Khwarazmians for a brief period, then lost to another Muslim, then reoccupied in 645/1247-8.[7] The regions of Tiberias, Ascalon and Baysān among others, were reoccupied in the same period[8] and some of these new Palestinian *iqṭā‘s* must have been given to the Baḥrīs, for when Aqṭāy al-Jamdār was murdered in 652/1254, the Baḥrīs fled to al-Nāṣir Yūsuf the ruler of Damascus, and al-Nāṣir demanded from al-Mu‘izz Aybak the formal cession of the Palestinian lands (the Sāhil) where the Baḥrī fiefs had been, and reinvested Baḥrī *amīrs* with these *iqṭā‘s*.[9] Baybars, during this period of exile, held half of Nābulus and Jīnīn. Nābulus had been one of the regions acquired by al-Ṣāliḥ Ayyūb in 644/1246-7 from the ruler of Damascus, al-Ṣāliḥ Ismā‘īl. Later Baybars and other Baḥrīs, on the pretext of visiting their *iqṭā‘s* in the areas of Nābulus and Gaza, deserted al-Nāṣir to join al-Mughīth, the ruler of al-Karak. Later still, in 657/1259, when al-Nāṣir had re-established his ascendancy in that area, the Baḥrīs returned to his service and Baybars was reconfirmed in his tenure of half Nābulus and Jīnīn.[10] There seems to be an implication in the chronicler's accounts of the above events that some *iqṭā‘s* implied some sort of *de facto* control of the lands in question, possibly they were administrative *iqṭā'ṣ* on the Seljuk model. Ṣarkhad was also held as an administrative *iqṭā'* under al-Nāṣir. But not all of Muslim Palestine was held by Baḥrīs. Jerusalem for instance, in 655/1256-7 was the *iqṭā'* of a certain Sayf al-Dīn Kabak (or Aybak) and from the context of the references to this *muqṭa'* it is clear that he had considerable control of the town and its region and was not simply the recipient of some of its revenue. He was in fact its *nā'ib* or *wālī* (governor).[11] *Iqṭā's* comprising the whole or part of a Palestinian town were obviously exceptional but we know from Ibn Abd al-Ẓāhir's chronicle that other Baḥrī *iqṭā's* were concentrated in the Gaza-*Sāḥil* area,[12] although Gaza itself was under a *wālī*. A further implication to be gleaned from the sources was that while Sayf al-Dīn Kabak seems to have resided on his *iqṭā'* at Jerusalem, it was more normal not to do so, but that there was nothing unusual in an *amīr* asking and getting permission *(dustūr)* to visit his *iqṭā'*. When one considers the prestige of the Baḥrīs in the period, the presumption must be that *iqṭā's* in the hinterland of Palestine were elite *iqṭā's*.

To a very large extent these observations remain true for the reigns of Quṭuz (657-8/1259-60) and Baybars (658-76/1260-77), that is that Palestinian *iqṭā'* is frequently referred to, it is highly coveted and we find instances of administrative *iqṭā'* co-existing with the more conventional fiscal *iqṭā'* in the same area. For instance, Nābulus (Baybars' former *iqṭā'*) remained a plum *iqṭā'* in this period. It was given to a very influential figure, Shams al-Din Āqūsh al-Burlī when Quṭuz made him *nā'ib* (governor) over Gaza and the coastal provinces. Later Baybars confirmed him in it and added Baysān to it. Later still after Āqūsh's downfall, a highly-valued *Wāfidī* (immigrant) *amīr*, Sayf al-Dīn Salār was given half the town as an *iqṭā'* of fifty (that is to say an *iqṭā'* which would be expected to produce fifty cavalrymen).[13] Equally Hebron during the reign of Baybars, had no *wālī*, as far as one can discover, but was assigned as *iqṭā' in toto* to the *nā'ibs* of al-Karak as a perquisite of office.[14]

One indication of the pressure from the *amīrs* to receive fiefs in Palestine from the sultan, is that when Baybars, early in his reign, in 661 1262-3 makes his first territorial gains from the Franks in the region of Nazareth and Mount Tabor he immediately grants these lands out in *iqṭā'*, and we must emphasise that it was an immediate distribution. As soon as Baybars had destroyed the church at Nazareth and abandoned his inconclusive foray against Acre, he summoned the *atābak* and the scribes of the chancery and had them sit up all night writing *manāshīr* (formal documents setting out the terms of the sultan's grant) and has the fifty-six documents in question distributed the next morning, together with other signs of royal favour. Doubtless it was necessary to purchase the loyalty of the *amīrs* before moving against al-Mughīth, the Ayyubid ruler at al-Karak.[15]

On the face of it there was an exact repeat performance of this emergency distribution of *iqṭā'* in 663/1264-5 in the area of Caesarea and Arsūf,[16] but on the face of it only. In 663/1264-5 the Mongols had attacked al-Bīra, a Mamluk fortress on the Euphrates. Advance detachments of the Mamluk army in Egypt were sent north post-haste to relieve the fortress, while Baybars and the main body of the army advanced out of Egypt at a more leisurely pace. While Baybars was in southern Palestine he heard that the threat to al-Bīra was over and he sensibly decided to use the large forces assembled under his command to attack the Frankish coastal cities. Casesarea was captured on 5 March and Arsūf was taken, probably, on 30 March. Both towns were destroyed to prevent their re-occupation by the Franks, but immediately this had been achieved, villages in the region were distributed among sixty *amīrs*. The general and formal preface to the charter in question and the lists of the names of the *amīrs* and of the names of the villages have been preserved in Ibn al-Furāt's chronicle, and many of the villages awarded in the document have been identified. The document and the related lists are of extraordinary interest. Among its many features of secondary interest we may single out the fact that most of the *amīrs* in the list of recipients can be identified, that the list follows an approximate order of seniority and political importance, that a number of *amīrs* who are mentioned by the chronicle as playing a prominent role in the two sieges are not on the list, while certain others are, including the army commanders at al-Bīra and the *nā'ibs* of Egypt, Damascus and al-Karak, although they were not on this expedition.

Among the sixty recipients on the list there were at least a dozen of the still very powerful Ṣāliḥī Baḥrī *amīrs*, though there were no less than eight of Baybars's own Ẓāhiri Mamluk *amīrs*. That is to say, the old guard, al-Ṣāliḥ Ayyūb's former Mamluks, are still prominent, but that even at this early stage in his reign, Baybars has lost no time in advancing his own Mamluks. But not all of those listed were Mamluk *amīrs*. Some, at least, were freeborn Kurdish *amīrs*, formerly in the employment of al-Nāṣir Yūsuf of Damascus, and many of them were Wāfidiyya, in particular Wāfidiyya from Bagdad. (Wāfidiyya is the term used to denote distinguished refugees coming into the Mamluk state and the service of the sultanate from beyond its frontiers.) The implication here and elsewhere in the chronicles of the period is that these immigrant notables were given a welcome and accorded an importance which they were not to enjoy under later sultans.[17] Among the office-bearers listed are the more prominent *nā'ibs*, the *atābak*, the *khazindār*, the *amīr silāḥ*, the two *silaḥdārs*, the *amīr jāndār* and his deputy the *amīr mihmandār* and the *ustādhdār*, but not the *amīr jamdār*, the *dawādār* nor either of the *ḥājibs*. This of course sheds some light on Mamluk ranking and which offices were considered not to be of great importance.

The chief feature of interest with respect to the villages granted is that none of them are actually on the coast. In particular, none of them is in the immediate vicinity of Arsūf.

But what has hitherto escaped emphasis by those who have studied this document is that the villages are not being distributed as *iqṭā'* at all. The document is quite explicit about this: they are being distributed as *mulk* (freehold tenure). That is to say, what is being granted out is not an assignment of revenue held for a limited period dependent on office and service of the state, revocable at the whim of the sultan, but allodial property, the land itself, and this may also be passed on to one's heirs. As the preamble says:-

> 'He (the sultan) thought that he should prefer them (the *amīrs*) to himself, distributing over them the rays coming from the light of his sun, so as to leave to their sons and their sons' sons something which would last to the end of time and endure forever. Thus the sons could live on his favour as their fathers had done.'

The documents of the grants themselves are referred to by the chronicler as *al-tawāqī' bi'l-tamlīk* (diplomas of ownership).

The 663 distribution was in a sense a repeat performance of the largess in 661 but in a more extreme form. Baybars, in lavishly alienating in perpetuity the territories around Caesarea and Arsūf, was responding to pressure from the *amīrs*. According to al-Maqrīzī's *Kitāb al-sulūk*, in doing so he was not acting thus from spontaneous generosity, but rather responding to a specific demand from the *amīrs* that he should do just this. Reading between the lines, and indeed in the lines of the inflated and conceited rhetoric of the preamble to the charter, I think we can discern two things. Firstly, as one can see from the passage quoted above, the Mamluk *amīrs* are worried about their future and about the future of their families. Some at least of them must have hoped that now that there was a Mamluk-controlled regime in power it might be possible to transmit their wealth and authority not to other Mamluks but to their own children. In the long run this hope was not to be fulfilled. On the other hand, the sultan Baybars himself clearly feels insecure, in particular about the theoretical basis of his right to rule. The charter's preamble suggests that his right rested partly on achievement, on his victories over the heathen Mongols and the infidel Franks. 'Fortune *(al-sa'da)* made him king.' In part it rested on his solicitude for his followers. 'He did not wish to be singled out from amongst them by receipt of a favour nor to enjoy by himself and appropriate exclusively a benefit won by their swords and obtained by their resolution. He thought that he would prefer them to himself.' The document hints at an almost contractual relationship between the sultan and his *amīrs*. This is a picture which the chroniclers' rather muddled accounts of Baybars's acclamation as sultan after the death of Quṭuz seem to confirm.[18]

In the later years of Baybars's reign after a series of successful purges of some of the more dangerous *amīrs* (among them Sanjar al-Ḥalabī and Āqūsh al-Muḥammadī) the balance shifted somewhat in the sultan's favour, but in the early years at least this dependent relationship with his Ṣāliḥī and Kurdish *amīrs* meant that there were bound to be anomalies in his distribution of the territories conquered in Syria and Palestine and in the operation of the *iqṭā'* system. Thus for instance the chronicles place great emphasis on the fact that when the *Amīr* Shihāb al-Dīn al-Qaymarī died, his son was allowed to inherit his *iqṭā'* of one hundred. Equally when another Palestinian *amīr*, Shujā al-Dīn, the *wālī* of Sarmīn, disappeared on a mission to the Franks, his *iqṭā'* was transferred to his brothers.[19] When 'Izz al-Dīn al-Ḥillī died in 667/1268-9 his son inherited an *iqṭā'* of forty horsemen.[20] Interestingly enough, when Baybars did move in 661/1262-3 against a powerful rival, 'Izz al-Dīn al-Dimyāṭī, and removed him from his *iqṭā'*, he sought to weaken possible resistance to his coup by allowing Dimyāṭī's Mamluks to remain on the *iqṭā'*.[21] Nor was the assignment of freehold property at Caesarea and Arsūf an isolated occurrence. In 666/1267-8, Ṭaybars al-Wazīrī and Sanjar al-Ḥamawī were each given a village in Palestine probably in the area of Jaffa or Ludd,[22] and on another occasion 'Alā' al-Dīn al-Ḥājj al-Ruknī was given two villages in Palestine to retire to.[23] The same procedure of handing over a freehold tenure was followed when Sharaf al-Dīn b. Abi 'l Qāsim was placed on retirement.[24] Not only did the powerful rivals of the sultan have to be propitiated, but the resources of Baybars's own favoured Ẓāhirī Mamluks had to be strengthened. Thus his most trusted lieutenant, Badr al-Dīn Bīlīk al-Khazindār was given the castle of al-Ṣubayba and the town of Banyās to hold as *mulk*, and Bīlī entered into a pact of homage with Baybars for it (an anomalous occurrence possibly inspired by the practice of Frankish knights).[25] Later on in the 690s/1290s the same area was given in *mulk* to Baydarā al-Ashrafī, a favourite of al-Malik al-Ashraf Khalīl b. Qalāwūn.[26] The situation was hardly more regular under Qalāwūn. In 680/1281-2 Qalāwūn came to terms with the rebel Shams al-Dīn Sunqur al-Ashqar and Sunqur was granted an amirate of six hundred cavalry including the *iqṭā's* of Afāmiya, Kafr Ṭāb, Antioch, al-Suwaydiyya, Bakās and Darkūsh. There can be no doubt in his case that '*iqṭā'*' is being used here not in any technical sense, but as a face-saving term denoting the *de facto* authority of Sunqur over a large area of northern Syria.[27]

Apart from the pressures to create special and irregular forms of tenure for rivals and supporters within the Mamluk state, a further source of anomalies was produced by the need to co-exist with the Franks. Instances of Frankish knights holding *iqṭā'* under the Mamluk sultans are by no means unknown. We have already noted the fact that while the hinterland of Arsūf and Caesarea was distributed as *mulk*, the coastal strip was not. Plausibly, I maintain, this was because the area remained in Frankish hands, albeit under Mamluk suzerainty. According to Ibn 'Abd al-Ẓāhir: 'While Baybars was at Caesarea (in 663) some Franks came and offered their submissio including a son of one of the princes. Baybars gave them *iqṭā'* and treated them favourably.' The phrasing of Ibn 'Abd al-Ẓāhir hardly allows any doubt that it is *iqṭā'* and not treaty negotiations which are being referred to here. If treaty negotiations had been in question, Ibn 'Abd al-Ẓāhir would certainly have known of it for it would almost certainly have been he or, if not he, then one of his colleagues in the chancery who would have had the responsibility of drafting any truce document. If there were any doubt however, a quite independent reference in an appendix of 'Izz al-Dīn Ibn Shaddād's life of Baybars should dispel it. The appendix in Ibn

Shaddād deals with those people who came into the sultan's service from outside the frontiers of his realm (i.e. Wāfidiyya). It consists largely of lists of émigrés from the Mongols, from Anatolia, from Bagdad and elsewhere, but there is a brief section on the Franks. In it Ibn Shaddād remarks:

> 'There came a *wafd* [a delegation seeking protection] to sultan [lacuna] from Ṣafad as well as the son of the lord of Arsūf and three hundred horsemen. They took Islam at Baybars's hand and he put them in the victorious *ḥalqa* and gave them excellent *iqṭā'*s of the *ajnād* [soldiers of the *ḥalqa*].'[28]

If Ibn Shaddād and Ibn 'Abd al-Ẓāhir are to be believed then, shortly before the Hospitallers were to lose Arsūf, a son of its former lord, John III, entered Baybars's service and was enfeoffed (presumably with the old Ibelin lands shortly to be occupied on the coast of Arsūf and Caesarea) and this relationship was formalised by being described as *iqṭā'* in the *ḥalqa*.

A vague precedent for this sort of arrangement may be found in the confrontation between John of Jaffa and Baybars in 661/1262-3 when instead of the normal procedures being observed for a treaty negotiation between formal equals, John of Jaffa submitted to the sultan and prostrated himself before him. He was then confirmed in his possession of the town by a *manshūr* document: the term *manshūr* is used among other things for charters granting *iqṭā'*, while the normal term for a treaty or truce document was a *hudna*.[29]

Apart from the case of Arsūf and the more ambiguous proceedings at Jaffa, there are two further cases known where Franks received *iqṭā'* from the Mamluks. First, after the fall of Ṣafad to Baybars in 664/1266 one of its knights apostatised and was given *iqṭā'*.[30] Secondly, after the fall of Tripoli in 688/1289 the sultan Qalāwūn gave the son of his old ally Guy Embriaco the town of Jubayl to hold in *iqṭā'*.[31] Parenthetically it should be pointed out that there are no certain cases in this period of the reverse procedure, of Muslims holding fiefs from Franks. There are two cases, cited in Jonathan Riley-Smith's *The feudal nobility and the Latin kingdom of Jerusalem, 1174-1277* of feudatories with partially Arab names, but these were probably Syrian Christians - or even Franks who had acquired Arab nicknames.[32] Although the Buhturid *amīrs* in the Gharb region of the Lebanon were certainly either Druzes or orthodox Muslims and copies of grants of fiefs to them by the Franks in 1255 and 1280 are given in Ṣāliḥ b. Yaḥyā's *Ta'rīkh Bayrūt*, all the documents this chronicle provides us with for this period dealing with grants of *iqṭā'* or fief contain so many glaring anomalies in dates and individuals referred to, and in their diplomatic that they were probably forged.[33]

A more common form of accommodation between Mamluk and Frank than the unusual cases discussed above was the partition treaty in which a certain designated area on their frontiers was left intact as a territorial unit, but its revenues were divided between the Mamluks and Frankish lords. Such treaties were concluded with the sultans for instance, by the Hospitallers of Margat (al-Marqab) in 655/1266-7, Cursat (al-Quṣayr) in 666/1268, Tortosa in 669/1271, Margat in 669/1271, Tripoli in 669/1271, Tyre in 669/1271, Tripoli in 680/1281, Acre in 683/1283, and Tyre in 684/1285. That of Tyre in 669/1271 is of particular interest for we have a subsequent document on the Frankish side discussing the necessity for arbitration over certain *casaux* (estates) and *gastines* (totally or partially abandoned land) and whether they fell under the partition.[34] The document implies that on the Muslim side it is the holders of *iqṭāʿ* who collect the revenue (in this case *muqṭaʿs* based on the Mamluk centre of government at Ṣafad). If the *muqṭaʿs* kept the revenue they collected (and this is not known) the presumption would be that in some areas at least, the revenues provided by an *iqṭāʿ* were identical with the traditional seigneurial revenues the Franks were accustomed to levy.

The nature of the revenues that a Mamluk or anyone else would normally collect from an *iqṭāʿ* is very far from clear. Rabie says that the conferment of *iqṭāʿ* gave the right to collect a limited number of taxes only, but he fails, I think, to identify convincing sources of regular revenue - he mentions the *marāʿī* tax (a tax on livestock going back to the ninth century) and the *hilālī* tax (an annual tax for licensing bakeries, shops etc.),[35] but there is no evidence that these were levied in thirteenth-century Syria. There are references to taxes on beer, wine and prostitutes which were collected in the thirteenth century by *muqṭaʿs*, and which were abolished by Baybars, but it seems unlikely to me at least that the armies of medieval Egypt and Syria were maintained wholly or largely on immoral earnings. A base tax on agricultural produce must be a necessity for a workable *iqṭāʿ* system.

Claude Cahen suggested that the *muqṭaʿ* collected *kharāj* but not *jizya*,[36] yet setting aside the *kharāj al-rātib* (the tax on orchards and vineyards) which was collected in this period, *kharāj* is employed very rarely and only vaguely in this period as a generic term meaning taxation. If *kharāj* was the main source of *iqṭāʿ* revenue, then it will have been paid in kind, and it will have been difficult for example for a Mamluk *amīr* employed in Egypt but holding Syrian *iqṭāʿ* to collect it or to convert into money. Moreover Gibb argued that in the early Ayyubid period during the rule of Saladin, when *kharāj* was collected on crops in Egypt, it was collected by the *muqṭaʿ* but forwarded by him to the state.[37]

So far we have confined ourselves to the examples of anomalies in the *iqṭāʿ* system of which there are an enormous number in this period. It remains to sketch in the more normal pattern of occupation. When a major Frankish castle or centre of government was taken, if it was not preventively destroyed, then large numbers of Royal Mamluks and other elite troops were moved in to garrison it. When Ṣafad was taken in 664/1266, fifty-four of Baybars's own Mamluks were moved in to occupy it. Both they and the *ajnad* were given *iqṭāʿ* in the region.[38] When Margat was taken in 684/1285, one hundred and fifty *ṭablkhānāh amīrs*, (that is *amīrs* of forty horsemen) and other *amīrs* were installed there together with specialist forces, and a large area including Kafr Ṭāb, Antioch and Latakia was set aside to provide for its garrison.[39] The port of Tripoli was destroyed in 688/1289 but subsequently ten *ṭablkhānāh amīrs* and fifteen *amīrs* of ten were posted in the area and given *iqṭā'*s there.[40] Acre also was destroyed and the region governed from Ṣafad, but a number of lesser Mamluk and non-Mamluk *amīrs* were given *iqṭā'*s in the environs.[41]

Beyond the environs of major strongholds, most of the *iqṭā'* in Syria and Palestine, like most of the minor posts in local government were held by the *ḥalqa*. In particular this was true of areas like Ba'labakk and al-Karak which had remained uninterruptedly in Muslim hands throughout the thirteenth century. Professor Ayalon in his 'Studies in the structure of the Mamluke Army' has singled out two elements in the *ḥalqa*; firstly the Wāfidiyya (to whom reference has already been made in this paper) and secondly, the *awlād al-nās* (literally, 'sons of the people', in fact sons of Mamluks who were given low-grade non-Mamluk commands and *iqṭā'*s).[42] I feel that it needs to be emphasised that the *ḥalqa* in this period was not solely comprised of these elements. Rather, as Poliak recognised, the term '*ḥalqa*' or '*ajnād al-ḥalqa*' (troops of the *ḥalqa*) is used to refer to all those soldiers in the service of the sultan who are neither Mamluk in origin, nor auxiliary troops like the irregular and occasional forces provided usually by the Arabs and Turcomans. In fact the *ḥalqa* in the late thirteenth century was probably the largest single element in the armies of the sultans. At the battle of Ḥimṣ (680/1281), for instance, they numbered at least four thousand.[43] All of the *ḥalqa* were freeborn. Some of them were *amīrs* or were in the service of *ḥalqa amīrs*. Particularly prominent among the *ḥalqa* at this time were the Qaymarī Kurdish *amīrs* and certain local dignitaries in Palestine including among them men like 'Imād al-Dīn b. Abī' l-Qāsim, Kamāl al-Dīn b. Shīth and Jamāl al-Dīn b. Nahār. A study of the names and careers of men like these reveals that they were not Wāfidiyya or *awlād al-nās*, but they were in the service of the Mamluk government in Palestine and held or received *iqṭā'*s there. It is likely that the term *mufradī* (pl. *mafārida*) is the term occasionally used to designate *ḥalqa amīrs*.

Some of the Turcoman tribes in Palestine were also included in the *ḥalqa*, not in the sense of being subsumed in the *ḥalqa* on campaign, but in the sense that they received *ḥalqa iqṭā'*s. They often performed patrol duties on the coasts of Syria and Palestine, and in such cases it is perfectly clear that the tenure of land in *iqṭā'* included the right to pasture one's flocks on it.[44]

Others of the *ajnād al-ḥalqa* who were not *amīrs* were maintained by and in the service of Mamluk *amīrs*. If we follow the career of a royal Mamluk, for instance Baybars al-Dawādār al-Manṣūrī, it is clear that as he moved from post to post his *iqṭā'* was changed.[45] Clearly the *amīr*'s own Mamluks followed the *amīr* to each new posting for otherwise there could be no continuity in training and in group loyalty to the master *(khushdāshiyya)* but the bulk of his levies from an *iqṭā'* were freeborn cavalrymen *(ajnād al-ḥalqa)* who would be transferred from master to master rather than from estate to estate. From Baybars al-Manṣūrī's account of his career it emerges incidentally that although he was already campaigning as an *amīr* of five in 663/1264-5, he was maintained by pay *(jāmakiyya)* and he was not given an *iqṭāʿ* or any portion of one by his *ustādh* (master), Qalāwūn, until 671/1272-3. Very likely most *iqṭāʿ* in Syria was held by the *ḥalqa*. *Iqṭāʿ* was used to maintain and reward Mamluk *amīrs* if they were employed on garrison duty in the provinces, but otherwise it does not seem to have had much importance for them save to indicate status. The inner ring of *amīrs* were so busily employed on state business that they can rarely have visited their *iqṭāʿ* estates and were so generously rewarded in other ways that they can have had little inclination to do so. What revenues they were allowed to collect from these estates is, as we have seen, open to speculation.

If the revenue an *iqṭāʿ* could supply a Mamluk was uncertain, it certainly provided no basis for the establishment of decentralized authorities and provincial loyalties that they could call upon. The two great revolts of the thirteenth century, by Sanjar al-Ḥalabī in 658/1260 and by Sunqur al-Ashqar in 678/1280, were launched by *amīrs* whose power-base lay not in their *iqṭāʿs* and their own Mamluks and *ajnād*, but in the office they both held, the *niyāba* of Damascus, and in the support of other Syrian officials. *Iqṭāʿ* was of much greater significance for the *amīrs* of the *ḥalqa*, where the grant of *iqṭāʿ* was often the formal acknowledgement by the central government that the recipient was the local power in the area and a confirmation of the latter's traditional standing there.[46]

Further we must not forget that much of Syria and Palestine was neither Mamluk *iqṭāʿ* nor *mulk* nor *ḥalqa iqṭāʿ*. Much land was held under *waqf*, a form of settlement of property used to endow trusts for religious and charitable purposes. This of course particularly applies to Palestine. There had always been extensive *waqfs* to support various institutions in Jerusalem. When Jaffa was taken by Baybars in 666/1268 much of its land was made into *waqf* and the same thing happened after the capture of Shaqīf Arnūn (Beaufort) and Acre.[47] In 660/1262 Baybars had actually converted some of the land held around Hebron as *iqṭāʿ* back to its former status as *waqf*.[48]

There are no broad and simple conclusions. Thirteenth-century Syria and Palestine were not like that. The original meaning of the word *iqṭāʿ* assigned to it by the Arab lexicographers is 'portion' and it is often used in the sources to mean something no more precise than that. *Iqṭāʿ* was used as a means of maintaining garrisons, as a mark of status, as a formal approval of a local notability, as a recognition of *de facto* political authority, as a loose equivalent of the term *wilāya*, and very likely even to designate Frankish fief tenure under Muslim suzerainty. Not all Mamluk *amīrs* held *iqṭāʿ*, not all land was under *iqṭāʿ*. After the accession of the sultan Baybars until the early decades of the fourteenth century (when *iqṭāʿ* was systematised in Egypt by the great cadastral surveys) the role of *iqṭāʿ* in the formation of the Mamluk system of government was probably quite small. Its main role seems to have been to maintain *amīrs* and soldiers who were not Mamluks. It did so by providing revenues, about the precise nature of which I, at least, am still very uncertain.

It may be felt that to some extent the fragmentary nature of the conclusions reached in this paper are a product of the severely restricted time-span considered, but it seems to me to be a very dangerous assumption that there is substantial continuity in Syrian institutions from Saladin to Baybars al-Bunduqdārī and further to the last days of the Circassian sultans - that the Islamic world in the Middle Ages was in some sense more monolithic and more resistant to change than its Christian neighbour.

This brings me to my penultimate observation - that it is as yet too early to attempt a useful, still less a definitive comparison between feudalism in the thirteenth-century kingdom of Jerusalem and the so-called system of *iqṭāʿ* in Ayyubid or Mamluk Syria. With regard to the problem of Islamic feudalism, the two poles of opinion are well represented by A. N. Poliak and by Claude Cahen. Poliak wrote of Muslim 'knights', their 'fiefs' and their seigneurial rights. Cahen has since denied the validity of this terminology, arguing that the state had ultimate control of the *iqṭāʿs*, that the tenure of an *iqṭāʿ* was in no sense contractual or dependent on a pact and that the holders of *iqṭāʿ* were a town-dwelling elite with little if any interest in the administration of their so-called 'fiefs'.

My own feeling is that the epithet 'feudal' cannot be decisively ruled out of court yet. As the researches of Joshua Prawer and Jonathan Riley-Smith have shown, the knights of the kingdom of Jerusalem tended to belong to a town-dwelling elite too. As this paper has suggested, there were occasionally contractual elements in thirteenth-century Muslim land-tenure, and some *amīrs* did reside on their *iqṭāʿs*, either because they were *ḥalqa amīrs*, or because, as at Nābulus or at al-Subayba, they were Mamluk *amīrs* exercising *de facto* authority over that territory.

In this study use of the chancery encyclopaedists has been avoided. The vast bureaucratic and meritocratic system that al-Qalqashandī so ponderously elaborated in *Ṣubḥ al-aʿshā* barely existed in the thirteenth century. In this context *Ṣubḥ al-aʿsha* reminds one of Borges's Chinese encyclopaedia in which animals are divided 'a) those that belong to the Emperor, b) embalmed ones, c) those that are trained, d) suckling pigs, e) mermaids, f) fabulous ones, g) stray dogs, h) those that are included in this classification, etc.'[49] Al-Qalqashandī's classifications are simply not useful. One suspects that he found the early history of the Baḥrī Mamluk sultanate as difficult to understand as we do.

ROBERT IRWIN

SHORT REFERENCES

A'lāq: Ibn Shaddād, *al-A'lāq al-khaṭīra fī dhikr umarā' al-Shām wa'l-Jazīra* (ed. S. Dahan), Damascus, 1963. B.M. MS. Or. Add. 23334.

Ayyubids: U. and M. C. Lyons and J. Riley-Smith, *Ayyubids, Mamlukes and Crusaders* Cambridge, 1971

BÉO: *Bulletin d'Études Orientales de l'Institut Français de Damas.*

BSOAS: *Bulletin of the School of Oriental and African Studies.*

Dhayl: al-Yūnīnī, *Dhayl mir'āt al-zamān*, Hyderabad, 1954-61.

EI2: *Encyclopaedia of Islam*, 2nd edition, Leiden, 1960.

Ibn ad-Dawādārī: *Die Chronik des Ibn ad-Dawādārī*, VIII (ed. U. Haarmann), Cairo, 1971.

Ibn al-Furāt: *Ta'rīkh Ibn al-Furāt*, VII (edd. C. K. Zurayk and N. Izzadin), Beirut, 1942; VIII (same eds.) Beirut, 1939.

JESHO: *Journal of the Economic and Social History of the Orient.*

JPOS: *Journal of the Palestine Oriental Society.*

Nujūm: Ibn Taghrībirdī, *al-Nujūm al-zāhira fī mulūk Miṣr wa'l Qāhira*, VII, Cairo, (n.d.).

Rabie: Hassanein Rabie, *The financial system of Egypt A.H. 564-741/ A.D. 1169-1341*, London, 1972.

RAO: *Recueil d'Archéologie Orientale.*

Rawḍ: Ibn 'Abd al-Ẓāhir, *al-Rawḍ al-zāhir fī sīrat al-Malik al-Ẓāhi*
Fatih: Istanbul, MS. Fatih 4367.
Sadeque: S. F. Sadeque, *Baybars I of Egypt*, Dacca, 1956.
Khowayter: Abdul Aziz al-Khowayter, *A critical edition of an unknown Arabic source for the life of al-Malik al-Ẓāhir Baybars* (unpbd. Ph.D. thesis, London, 1960).

Rawḍa: Ibn Shaddād, *al-Rawḍa al-zāhira fi'l-sīra al-ẓāhira*, Edirne, MS. Selimiye 1507.

RHC: *Recueil des Historiens des Croisades.*

Sulūk: al-Maqrīzī, *Kitāb al-sulūk li-ma'rifat duwal al-mulūk*, I (ed. M. Mustafa Ziada), Cairo, 1956-8.

Zubda: Baybars al-Manṣūrī, *Zubdat al-fikra fī ta'rīkh al-hijra*, B.M. MS. Or. Add. 23325.

1. Mustafa M. Ziada, 'The Mamluk Sultans to 1293', in *A history of the Crusades* (ed.-in-chief K. M. Setton), II, 2nd edn., Madison, 1969, at p.755.

2. A. N. Poliak, *Feudalism in Egypt, Syria, Palestine, and the Lebanon 1250-1900*, London, 1939, 18 ff.

3. Cl. Cahen, IḲṬĀʿ, *EI2*.

4. Rabie, 26-72.

5. D. Ayalon, 'The system of payment in Mamluk military society', *JESHO*, I, 1957-8, 49-50.

6. E. Ashtor, *Histoire des prix et des salaires dans l'Orient médiéval*, Paris, 1969, 373-4.

7. *Aʿlāq*, III, 235; *Sulūk*, I, ii, 318.

8. *Ayyubids*, II, 45-6; *Aʿlāq*, III, 129, 262; *Sulūk*, I, ii, 327-8.

9. Cl. Cahen, "'La chronique des Ayyoubides' d'al-Makin b. al-Amid", *BÉO*, XV, 1955, 164; *Sulūk*, I, ii, 393.

10. Cahen, "'La chronique des Ayyoubides'", at p.169; *Dhayl*, III, 240-1; Ibn ad-Dawādārī, VIII, 37; *Nujūm*, VII, 97-8, 99; *Sulūk*, I, ii, 415.

11. *Nujūm*, VII, 44-5; *Dhayl*, I, 51.

12. *Aʿlāq*, III, 266; *Sulūk*, I, ii, 392.

13. Ibn Wāṣil, *Mufarrij al-kurūb fī akhbār Bani Ayyūb*, MS. Paris ar. 1702, f. 400a; *Zubda*, f. 50b; *Sulūk*, I, ii, 468.

14. *Rawḍ*, Fatih, f. 514a (Khowayter, III, 1158); *Aʿlāq*, III, 242.

15. *Sulūk*, I, ii, 489-90; *Rawḍ*, Sadeque, 175-8 (Khowayter, II, 460-2).

16. On this episode, see *Zubda*, ff. 70a-71b; *Dhayl*, II, 318; Ibn ad-Dawādārī, VIII, 108-14; *Ayyubids*; I, 98-104, II, 78-82, 208-210, 249; F. M. Abel, 'La liste des donations de Baibars en Palestine d'après la charte de 663 H. (1265)', *JPOS*, XIX, 1939, 38-44. It is probable that the original source for all the Arabic chronicles for this episode was Ibn ʿAbd al-Ẓāhir, *al-Rawḍ al-zāhir*, but the relevant passage does not seem to have survived.

17. D. Ayalon, 'The Wafidiya in the Mamluk kingdom', *Islamic Culture*, XXV, 1951, 89-104.

18. See, for example, *Sulūk*, I, ii, 436; *Nujūm*, VII, 83-4; 'Les Gestes des Chiprois', *RHC, Documents arméniens*, II, 165-6.

19. *Rawḍ*, Sadeque, 175-8 (Khowayter, II, 460-2); *Sulūk*, I, ii, 508-9.

20. *Rawḍ*, Fatih, f. 132b (Khowayter, III, 1161).

21. *Rawḍ*, Sadeque, 186 (Khowayter, II, 473).

22. *Sulūk*, I, ii, 565.

23. *Rawḍa*, ff. 201b-202b.

24. *Dhayl*, I, 318.

25. *Rawḍ*, Sadeque, 111, Fatih, f. 9b (Khowayter, II, 366-7); *A'lāq*, III, 144; *Dhayl*, I, 452-3; II, 107; III, 263; IV, 106; Ibn al-Furāt, VII, 93.

26. A. Moberg, *Ur 'Abd allāh Ibn 'Abd eẓ-Ẓâhir's Biografi över Sultanen el-Melik el-Aśraf Ḫalīl*, Lund, 1902, 29-39.

27. *A'lāq*, f. 92b; *Sulūk*, I, iii, 687: *Nujūm*, VII, 301.

28. *Rawḍ*, Fatih, f. 71a (Khowayter, III, 1058); *Rawḍa*, f. 246a; *Ayyubids*, I, 90; II, 72; *Sulūk*, I, ii, 528.

29. *Rawḍ*, Sadeque, 139 (Khowayter, II, 407); *Zubda*, ff. 48b-49a; *Ayyubids*, I, 52-3; II, 43-4; al-'Aynī, *'Iqd al-jumān*, in *RHC, Hist. or.*, II, 216-7.

30. *Rawḍ*, Fatih, f. 85b (Khowayter, III, 1082); *Sulūk*, I, ii, 547.

31. Ibn al-Furāt, VIII, 80.

32. Jonathan (S. C.) Riley-Smith, *The feudal nobility and the kingdom of Jerusalem*, London, 1973, 10.

33. This problem is too complex to be more than noted here, but the relevant documents may be found in Ṣāliḥ b. Yaḥyā, *Tārīḫ Bayrūt* (edd. Francis Hours and Kamal (S.) Salibi), Beirut, 1969, Kamal S. Salibi, *Maronite historians of medieva[l] Lebanon*, Beirut, 1959; C. Clermont-Ganneau, 'Deux chartes des croisés dans les archives arabes', *RAO*, VI, 1903-5, 1-20.

34. *Rawḍ*, Fatih, f. 153a (Khowayter, III, 1196); G. L. Fr. Tafel and G. M. Thomas, *Urkunden zur älteren Handels - und Staatsgeschichte der Republik Venedig*, III, Vienna, 1856-7 (repr. Amsterdam, 1964), 398-400; J. Richard, 'Un partage de seigneurie entre Francs et Mamlouks', *Syria*, XXX, 1953, 72-82

35. Rabie, 41.

36. Cl. Cahen IḲṬĀʻ, *EI2*.

37. H.A.R. Gibb, 'The armies of Saladin' in *Studies on the civilization of Islam*, Boston (Mass.), 1962, at p.75.

38. *Aʻlāq*, III, 150; *Nujūm*, VII, 139; *Dhayl*, II, 343.

39. Ibn ʻAbd al-Ẓāhir, *Tashrīf al-ayyām wa'l-ʻuṣūr fī sīrat al-Malik al-Manṣūr* (ed. Murād Kāmil), Cairo, 1961, 80-1.

40. Ibn al-Furāt, VIII, 90; Ṣāliḥ b. Yaḥyā, *Tārīḫ Bayrūt*, 71-2.

41. Ibn al-Dawādārī, VIII, 313.

42. D. Ayalon, 'Studies on the structure of the Mamluk army', II, *BSOAS*, XV, 1953, 448-51.

43. *Sulūk*, I, iii, 693.

44. *Rawḍa*, f. 241a.

45. On the early stages of Baybars al-Manṣūrī's career, see *Zubda*, ff. 69b-70a, 78a, 151b-152b, 154a, 157a-b; E. Ashtor, 'Étude sur quelques chroniques mamloukes', *Israel Oriental Studies*, I, Tel Aviv, 1971, 272-7.

46. For an instance of a non-Mamluk local man holding such *iqṭāʻ*, see Ibn al-Furāt, VIII, 2.

47. *Rawḍ*, Fatih, ff. 102b, 105b (Khowayter, III, 110, 114); *Rawḍa*, ff. 193b-195a, 257a-270b; Ibn al-Furāt, VIII, 121-2; *Nujūm*, VII, 121; Mujīr al-Dīn, *Kitāb al-uns al-jalīl bi taʻrīkh al-Quds waʻl-Khalīl*, Cairo, A.H. 1283, 433-5; E. Sivan, *L'Islam et la croisade*, Paris, 1968, 173.

48. *Rawḍ*, Sadeque, 114 (Khowayter, II, 371); *Sulūk*, I, ii, 445.

49. J. L. Borges, *Other inquisitions*, New York, 1966, 108.

Scenes of daily life from Mamluk miniatures

Some words should first be said about the general characteristics and style of Mamluk painting before looking at the more particular aspects of costume and genre depictions shown in this Ḥarīrī MS. which is in the British Museum. In art history there has always been an oscillation between realism and abstraction expressing the differences between the visual and mental concepts in art. This swing may be observed in Arab painting where the lively vigorous paintings of the earlier Mesopotamian school give way to the rather wooden and lifeless flat-toned depictions of the Mamluk school. This new phase of Arab painting was primarily concerned with line and colour patterns. (A modern comparison might profitably be made with the paintings produced by the Fauvist movement early this century).

The change of spirit is partly to be explained by the impact of the Mongol invasions and partly by the type of society which produced these works of art. In the thirteenth century the Mongols under Hülegü invaded Syria and annexed Antioch, but they were finally repulsed at ʿAyn Jālūt in 1260. This fact was of great importance to the arts. Not only were Egypt and Syria able to continue in relatively peaceful prosperity unravaged by the invaders but they provided a potential haven of refuge for those artisans and craftsmen who probably fled from the occupied Eastern territories. Richard Ettinghausen has made the point that artists from Mosul fled before the Mongols thus bringing certain North Iraqi mannerisms to Mamluk Egypt.[1]

Many of the faces depicted in miniatures indicate a Far Eastern origin. The eyes which are usually almond-shaped and slightly slanting, the thin arched eyebrows, and the mouth which is normally portrayed as small with curved upper-lips all point to a facial type which I would be inclined to call Mongoloid. The drooping moustache and the thin black beards are in my opinion further pointers to this type. The costumes also show obvious signs of Eastern influence particularly in the caps and headgear. According to an eminent art historian however, 'the results of the Mongol invasion only supporte an evolution corresponding to the general trend of Egyptian art which was always ready to look to Muslim Asia for artistic stimuli.'[2] And this statement must be given close consideration when one considers that in architecture, for example, Ibn Ṭūlūn's mosque in Cairo is based on the plan of the Great Mosque at Sāmarrā to a very marked extent. Further examples in other art forms are the continuation of Iraqi styles in Tulunid pottery owing to the importation of potters from that country, and Fatimid ivory carving where ʿAbbasid traditions were followed and cultural contacts between the two courts were close.

The second factor for the change of spirit was the type of society which produced these works. The Mamluk state was a feudal society where every individual had his place clearly marked out in the hierarchy. There was a complicated system of precedence at court and society became much more inflexible than before. Mamluk painting reflects this static type of society and formality to a very great extent. The art of the Mamluks could perhaps be said to be the most rigidly composed art produced by the Arabs. Whether the Mamluk state was more rigid than the late ʿAbbasid period is debatable but it possibly had a more deadening influence on art and literature.

The manuscript which is here considered is representative of the high-point of the Baḥrī Mamluk school of painting. It is number Add.22114 in the British Museum and was probably produced in Syria about 1300. It has eighty-three miniatures all of which are extremely well-preserved and these miniatures give a good insight into the life and customs of the times. Its paintings are particularly close to the Paris *Kalīla wa-Dimna* (arabe 3467) and this is shown most clearly in the facial representations. The two manuscripts are also close in the depictions of the costume patterns particularly those of the 'scroll-fold' type to be explained later. The Paris work is probably to be dated to the mid-fourteenth century as it is very close to a *Kalīla wa-Dimna* in Oxford which is dated 1354 (Pococke 400). There are however analogies in the British Museum manuscript under discussion with a work entitled *The Banquet of the Physicians* (now in the Biblioteca Ambrosiana in Milan) which is dated 1272. It would seem therefore that the Ḥarīrī manuscript under discussion should be considered somewhere between the two Paris and Oxford *Kalīla wa-Dimna* manuscripts, and the Milan manuscript, giving a probable date of about 1300 AD. It is probably of Syrian origin as its iconography bears close resemblances to the Syrian iconography of the 1222 *Maqāmāt* of Ḥarīrī in the Bibliothèque Nationale (arabe 6094).

Genre scenes were popular subjects for illumination and this Ḥarīrī manuscript contains a rich variety. There are scenes of theft and scenes of the hunt depicted. Trials before *qāḍīs* and before rulers and governors, banquets with musicians, drinking parties, scenes in libraries, pharmacists' shops, tents, camps on journeys and pilgrimages are all shown, as are inns, mosques, and funeral scenes. There are also scenes in bed and at wedding feasts, as well as in boats and at school.

There is in addition a wide variety of costume and clothing shown. Military or court figures are often shown wearing the *ṭirāz* or honorific formula on their sleeves. Originally this was probably reserved for those who held an *iqṭā'*, but in the miniatures it has probably simply become a decoration. The materials which are sometimes portrayed with what Holter has called 'Schnörkelfalten'[3] or with what others have called 'scroll folds' is probably meant to portray a material like watered silk. Mayer suggested that the word *mumawwaj* (i.e. with wavy lines) may indicate a material such as watered silk.[4] He goes on to state that a certain ʿUthmān b. Jaqmaq received a satin coat with a pattern of wavy lines or *aṭlas mutammar* (cf. the German for satin which is *Atlas*). Al-Maqrīzī(quoted again by Mayer) defines this material as 'Alexandrian silk woven with gold thread'. This is probably the kind of rich material, which is portrayed in Mamluk illuminations. The type of headgear which occurs most frequently in Mamluk manuscripts is the *sharbūsh*. This marked an *amīr* of the Baḥrī Mamluks and was 'a stiff cap trimmed with fur, rising to a slightly triangular front'.[5]

Ecclesiastical costume is portrayed by the *ʿimāma*, or turban which often was very long. The *ṭarḥa*, or scarf was worn over it and the neck, falling on to the shoulders. In this manuscript one of the miniatures depicts Abū Zayd preaching in the mosque at Samarqand. As a *khaṭīb* he is shown wearing black and the use of this colour has probably to be seen in a political context. Sultan Baybars installed a member of the ʿAbbasid family as a puppet caliph in Cairo in 1261 thereby continuing the fiction of the caliphate. Perhaps the use of this colour indicates knowledge of this fact particularly since Samarqand was the area from which the ʿAbbasids traditionally gained their support.

The women are usually shown wearing *qumṣān* (sing. *qamīs*), or chemises, which reached to the knees. Below this were worn *sarāwīl*, or long trousers. Over the whole person was the *izār*, or wrap. These wraps and the men's turbans were coloured distinctively for Christians, Jews and Samaritans, but the colours shown in the manuscript are not necessarily significant and are probably to be regarded as the expression of the artist's keen sense of colour and pattern. The *ʿiṣāba*, or piece of cloth, was worn round the hair and was worn under the *izār*.

The men are depicted wearing bright leggings and long, richly patterned coats or gowns with gold arm-bands and gold borders on the hem and the sleeves of their garments. Their white turbans are sometimes shown with a *rafraf* or tail-piece. Turbans of many other kinds occur however. Only slaves, who did not have a right to wear a turban, are shown wearinq felt hats.

A keen sense of observation may be observed in the representations of animals. This truth to life is often lacking in the paintings of the human beings. This has been noted by many scholars and appears to be an inherent Semitic trait. The Mamluk artists did not extend their rigid treatment to the depictions of animals as they did to the representations of human beings. But it must be pointed out that many of the painstaking representations of flying birds in this manuscript are intended purely for a decorative purpose.

In addition to the 'scroll-fold' type of decoration there are also two further types of costume patterns. One type is of geometric designs formed most often from the square or hexagon. The second type is of tendril and floral designs. The 'scroll-fold' decoration may be considered as the epitome of the Mamluk style of painting although this ornamentation appeared in the Vienna Galen manuscript (mid-thirteenth century from Mosul). The probable connection with the school of Mosul has already been noted and these Mamluk patterns must therefore be understood as an extension of that school. This manuscript has a particularly rich variety of geometric patterns using the hexagon most frequently.

DUNCAN HALDANE

1. R. Ettinghausen, *Arab Painting*, London, 1962, 145.

2. H. Buchthal, 'Three Illustrated Hariri manuscripts in the British Museum', *Burlington Magazine* 77 (1940), 152.

3. K. Holter 'Die Frühmamlukische Miniaturenmalerei', *Die Graphischen Künste*, N.F., 2, 1937, 8.

4. L. A. Mayer, *Mamluk Costume*, Geneva, 1952, 14, n.4.

5. *Ibid*, 27.

A Catalogue description of ADD.22114 in the British Library

Title: The Maqamat of al-Hariri

Date: About 1300

Origin: Probably Syria

Artist or Scribe: Unknown

Number of miniatures: 83. Generally they are of a horizontal size filling the width of the page.

1854-56 Catalogue description:
'Makamat al-Hariri, a classical work of fiction in Arabic (written in a fine hand of the 14th century and ornamented) with curious miniatures, eighty-four in number. 14th cent. Quarto.'

My description: 186 folios; size of the book, 20.3 x 28 cms.; size of the written page, 16 x 24 cms.; size of the outer margin, 19 x 26.7 cms.; 13 lines per folio. Medium quality cream non-watermarked paper, not highly glazed.
Black ink with red rubrics. Some titles and rosettes in gold.
Medium regular naskh of high calligraphic quality.
Recent red leather cover tooled in gold with gold *shamsiyya* and *lisan*.
No colophon. The seal on folio 186 verso is indecipherable.

A Bibliography of known reproductions of the miniatures

Buchthal, H. 'Painting of Syrian Jacobites in its relation to Byzantine and Islamic art', *Syria* 20 (1939), pl.XXIV ($f55^r$).

Buchthal, H. 'Three illustrated Hariri manuscripts in the British Museum', *Burlington Magazine* 77 (1940), pls.IIA ($f94^r$), C ($f79^v$), E ($f68^r$).

Ettinghausen, R. *Arab Painting*, London, 1962, 146 ($f94^r$).

Mayer, L. A. *Mamluk Costume*, Geneva, 1952, pl.XVIII 1($f68^r$), 2($f94^r$), pl.XIX 2($f135^v$).

Rice, D. S. 'The oldest illustrated Arabic manuscript', *Bulletin of the School of Oriental and African Studies*, 22 (1959), pl.6($f21^r$).

'Deacon or drink: some paintings of Samarra re-examined', *Arabica* 5(1958), pl.VIII ($f26^r$).

Rice, D. T. *Islamic Art*, London, 1965. Fig.141 ($f96^r$).

Islamic Painting, Edinburgh, 1971. Fig.27 (b) ($f132^r$).

Fig.1.

This miniature belongs to the fifteenth *maqāma* and depicts Abū Zayd refusing food from al-Ḥārith. The most notable feature is the way the hanging curtain is shown. This is probably a continuation of Byzantine traditions but also is comparable to the way the sky is often portrayed by Mamluk artists.

Fig.2.

A caravan en route from Damascus to Baghdād (*maqāma* of Sinjār). The fruit strewn on the ground is a typical Mamluk motif. The tree is possibly a sycamore or cypress.

Fig.3.

A merchant's wedding feast at Sinjār. As there are only males present this scene most probably represents the *hurūba* or flight. This ceremony took place on the morning after the wedding and lasted the whole day. It was expressly for the bridegroom and his companions. (E. W. Lane, *The modern Egyptians*, London, 1890, 158.) It was the equivalent to our stag party.

Fig.4.

Abū Zayd and the narrator at Naṣībīn. The building on the right consists of a high brick wall with an adjoined pillar. This probably is the surround of a doorway. Note the dome and what appears to be a funnel or chimney in brick. This is probably meant to represent an air-vent by means of which the north winds were guided down into the rooms which were kept cool and dark. The white spirals and lines may indicate a plaster surface.

Fig.5.

The two heroes and their companions in a boat on the River Euphrates. River boats draw more water at the bows than the stern on account of the liability of running aground. This would be a representation of the *sumayriyya* which was of Iraqi origin.

Fig.6.

The *khān*, or inn at Wāsiṭ. The composition of this miniature is highly representative of the Mamluk style with its rigid divisions.

Fig.7.

The *maqāma* of Ramla contains this painting of al-Ḥārith on his way to Mecca on the pilgrimage. Note the palanquin and the way the tail of the camel is depicted. This latter feature is found in the Mamluk Harīrī MS. in the Nationalbibliothek, Vienna.

Fig.8.

Abū Zayd, as a *faqīh*, instructing boys in school at Aleppo. The shape of the writing tablet is derived from that of the ancient classical writing tablet. E. Herzfeld in 'Die Tabula Ansata in der islamischen Epigraphik und Ornamentik', *Der Islam* 6, 1915-16, 192-3 has pointed out the important role these tablets played in the cult of the dead in Ancient Egypt.

The Crusading policy of King Peter I of Cyprus, 1359-1369

In October 1365 a fleet under the command of King Peter I of Cyprus sailed into Alexandria harbour and taking the authorities completely by surprise captured the city. A few days later, on the approach of an army from Cairo, it withdrew to Cyprus laden with booty.

This feat of arms marked the dramatic climax of Peter's military activities and was perhaps the most notable blow struck at the Mamluk empire by a Christian army at any time in its history. The ten years during which Peter occupied the throne of Cyprus saw an unprecedented burst of aggression from his base in what since 1291 had been the principal outpost of western Christendom in the eastern Mediterranean: Turkish shipping had been cleared from the seas; in 1361 the port of Satalia (Antalya) had been conquered, and then in 1362-1365 Peter himself was in the West to recruit the army with which he was to attack Egypt. The closing years of his reign witnessed a series of negotiations between Cyprus and the Mamluks, interspersed with raids along the coasts of Syria and Egypt from Ayas to Alexandria, and a second royal visit to the West. In January 1369 Peter was murdered by a group of his vassals, and peace was concluded in 1370.

Historians have generally taken the view that in 1365 Peter intended to win back the kingdom of Jerusalem of which he was titular king, either by conquest or by exchanging it for Alexandria and other acquisitions in Egypt. According to the commonly held opinion, Peter was 'dominated by one ruling passion, the prosecution of war against the infidel';[1] his expedition was 'a serious crusade to reconquer the Holy Land',[2] although 'it was the spirit of chivalry, rather than political thinking, which animated the expedition'.[3] In retrospect we can see that if Peter believed he could restore the kingdom of Jerusalem, he was grossly mistaken in his understanding of military realities and his crusade was indeed an anachronism. Part of the difficulty with Peter's reign - a difficulty which has not received the consideration it demands - is that the sources on which these views are based are not sober, impartial works of scholarship, but blatant propaganda - *excitatoriae* for his or for later crusades or *apologiae* for his actions. In particular, we may regard with suspicion the attempts by Philip of Mézières to ascribe to Peter the same motives and ambitions as he himself had, and we must remember that William of Machaut and his audience were as much interested in idealised chivalry as in historical truth. Given these shortcomings, it is now necessary to try to look behind the sources and ask, what was Peter trying to achieve? was he really the crusading enthusiast, bent on refounding the Latin kingdom, or did he have some other, more modest and more practical aim? The reign can conveniently be divided into three: the anti-Turkish measures of the years 1359-1362, the visit to the West and the Alexandria campaign, 1362-1365, and the raids and negotiations of 1366-1369. Peter's policies in each of these periods will be examined in turn in an attempt to answer these questions.

Peter's first major achievement was the capture of Satalia - probably then the most important port on the southern coast of Asia Minor - in August 1361. In the following years the local Turkish rulers were placed under tribute, Turkish coastal strongholds raided, and Turkish shipping driven off the seas. Repeated attempts to recapture Satalia were repulsed, and the Cypriots continued to hold it until in 1373 they handed it back to its former ruler rather than let it fall into the hands of the Genoese.[4] There was nothing novel in Peter's programme: there had been a Cypriot attempt to capture Satalia in the first decade of the thirteenth century,[5] and some evidence survives for the Turkish rulers paying tribute to Peter's father, Hugh IV, who himself had won what was evidently a major naval victory over them in about 1337.[6] The expedition of 1361 can best be understood in the light of Leontios Makhairas's statement[7] that it followed a Turkish attack on Cyprus: Turkish naval power was growing and decisive action was needed to counter it; Peter therefore re-asserted Christian mastery of the seas and so not only saved Cyprus from raids, but protected the all-important shipping lanes; in addition he seized the key Turkish port, thus providing a potentially useful Christian-controlled staging post for shipping bound for Cyprus and obtaining one of the most important outlets for the trade of central Asia Minor. Peter's policy is therefore evidence of an awareness that for both military and commercial reasons the Turks and in particular Turkish naval power had to be kept in check. This awareness had led to the Cypriot involvement in the various leagues which from the early 1330s were directed against Turkish positions in the Aegean. In 1334, following the preaching of a crusade in 1333, a force consisting of Papal, Venetian, French, Byzantine, Hospitaller and Cypriot ships defeated a Turkish navy, and there is some evidence that the Hospitallers, Byzantines and Cypriots went on to attack the Turkish-held port of Smyrna (Izmir).[8] Ten years later, in 1344, in response to a crusade preached in 1343, a combined Papal, Venetian, Hospitaller and Cypriot fleet succeeded in capturing Smyrna, and it appears that from then until Peter's reign, Cyprus more or less continuously supported its defence.[9] Both Venice and the Knights of St. John had good reason to curb Turkish expansion in the Aegean: in both cases their lands were threatened, and the Venetian route to

Constantinople and the Black Sea was jeopardised. Cypriot interests were less directly affected by changes in the Aegean, but Hugh IV's membership of these leagues was doubtless motivated as much by the desire to protect the sea-link to the West, as by the desire to remain on good terms with the other participants. Although the capture of Satalia was not the work of an international league,[10] Peter I's behaviour should be seen as the natural continuation and extension of these earlier policies.

If Peter's capture of Satalia in 1361 was in accord with past policies, his journey to the West in 1362 was a break with tradition. Never before had a crowned king of Cyprus visited Europe. As to the reasons for his journey, Leontios Makhairas, who gives only a passing reference to the suggestion that Peter hoped to recover Jerusalem, conveys the impression that he was going in answer to a papal summons to defend himself against his nephew's claim to the throne of Cyprus.[11] Hugh, the son of Peter's elder brother, was living in the West and had asserted his rights in 1360 when a Cypriot embassy arrived at the court of Pope Innocent VI to announce Peter's accession.[12] Whatever the legal merits of Hugh's claim, the Cypriots seem not to have wavered in their support for Peter. In 1361 a second Cypriot embassy arranged a composition by which Hugh was to receive a generous apanage in Cyprus in return for the recognition of his uncle as king.[13] From papal letters of November 1362, it would appear that the new pope, Urban V, had accepted the principle of a composition, though there was still disagreement over the precise terms.[14] But contrary to Leontios's statements, the papal letters surviving from these years give no indication that Peter had been summoned to appear in person,[15] and it is likely that the dispute could have been handled by his procurators. If Peter was not under papal summons, we can only assume that his main intention in going to the West was the organisation of a crusade. He arrived at Avignon at the end of March 1363, and at once (31 March) the pope ordered the preaching of the cross for an expedition to begin in March 1365. Evidently preliminary arrangements were well under way: King John of France was immediately named captain-general,[16] and in this connection it is doubtless significant that Peter's embassy of 1361 had made contact with him.[17] It is nevertheless possible that Peter's crusading initiative and his capture of Satalia were partly intended to ingratiate himself with the papacy and so gain papal support in his conflict with his nephew,[18] but the fact that he persisted with his crusade after the dispute had been settled proves that this explanation by itself is insufficient to account for his visit to Europe.

Although no king of Cyprus had ever before visited the West, Cypriot ambassadors had frequently gone there to discuss projected crusades and, on occasion, may have provided the impetus for renewed crusading activity. There is evidence that Lambertino, the bishop of Limassol who was in the West in 1341, was the prime mover of the negotiations which prepared the way for the Smyrna crusade of 1344;[19] though Cyprus seems to have been slow to join the crusading league of 1333-1334, it may be relevant to note that Cypriot ambassadors were at the papal court immediately before the crusade-encyclicals of 1333 were issued.[20] More to the point, Peter unquestionably recognised the limitations of Cypriot military power and the consequent need for help from the West if a major expedition was to be launched. This premise had lain behind Henry II's memorandum on the subject of the crusade to the Council of Vienne in 1311 and the advice submitted to the papacy by Cypriot ambassadors in 1323.[21] It is likely that the same consideration may have influenced Hugh IV's decision to marry his eldest son to a daughter of Louis, duke of Bourbon. who throughout the period from the Council of Vienne to the outbreak of war with England in the mid-1330s had been the most consistent enthusiast for crusading proposals among the French nobility.[22]

Peter's opportunities for recruitment in the West seemed good. The truce of Brétigny in 1360 followed by the treaty of Calais of the same year marked the formal cessation of hostilities between England and France. Peter could therefore hope for support from noblemen who had acquired a taste for warfare, and from unemployed soldiers of fortune and their bands. For his part, Pope Urban saw in the crusade a chance to rid France of the free companies.[23] But the adherence of the French king may well have been of doubtful value. His participation may have encouraged others to take the cross, but the instability of peace in France following the truce of Brétigny and the exhaustion of the financial resources of the crown cannot have been auspicious. Indeed, it may be asked whether King John was not merely hoping to use the clerical taxes raised for the crusade to pay off his ransom.[24] In the event, his death early in 1364 put an end to the participation of French royalty in the campaign, and though it may have led to the withdrawal of some of his subjects from the expedition, the danger that the crusade might fail to take place because of the king's commitments at home, or that it might founder because of some disagreement with the king of Cyprus, no longer existed. Although Peter spent over two years in the West recruiting and organising his expedition, it is probable that, as Philip of Mézières was to record, he was disappointed by the response.[25] His forces eventually set sail from Venice in June 1365 and made a rendezvous at Rhodes with a fleet bringing the contingent from Cyprus. We cannot be certain of the relative sizes of the two armies, but it is perhaps significant that all the sources are agreed that the Cypriot fleet contained substantially more ships.[26] It is possible therefore that, for all Peter's efforts, the force which sacked Alexandria in October 1365 consisted in the main of his own Cypriot vassals and retainers.

For Peter's crusading fleet anchored at Rhodes in 1365 there were several potential goals. We have ample cause to believe that its destination was kept secret until after it had departed for the final stage of its voyage, but when the decision to go to Alexandria was taken is a matter for conjecture; probably it had been Peter's intention throughout.[27] A campaign in the Aegean was ruled out as seems clear from the tenor of a papal letter of April 1365 to the Emperor John V Palaeologus, and there is also evidence that Peter's allies, the Hospitallers, were anxious not to re-open hostilities with the local Turkish *amīrs*.[28] Peter had gone to considerable trouble and expense in preparing his crusade, and despite the precedents of the expeditions of 1334 and 1344 he had probably always intended it to be directed to an area where Cypriot interests would be more immediately affected. The choice of targets was still wide. First there was southern Asia Minor. Peter could have followed up his success of 1361, but his brother, John, prince of Antioch, who had acted as regent during his absence, had completed the work of destroying Turkish shipping and forcing the Turks to pay tribute.[29] Another possibility was Cilician Armenia. Here Peter who had already taken over the defence of Gorhigos,[30] perhaps the only Armenian port of any consequence not then in Mamluk hands, could have combined with the Armenians in a joint effort to push the Mamluks out of Cilicia and advance into northern Syria. The idea of an invasion of Syria via Armenia had been discussed by various crusade-propagandists in the early fourteenth century and, for a number of military, economic or religious reasons, almost universally rejected.[31] But it is also likely that in 1365 the existing Armenian regime would not co-operate: an anti-Latin faction was in power, and Peter was probably committed to installing his illegitimate kinsman, the pro-Latin Leo of Lusignan, as king.[32] The remaining alternative was a direct assault on the Mamluks either in Syria or in Egypt.

The origins of the idea that 'Jerusalem could be won on the banks of the Nile' are traceable to the twelfth century.[33] In the thirteenth there had been two major expeditions to Egypt, the Fifth Crusade and St. Louis's first crusade, in the course of both of which the possibility of exchanging the Muslim-held parts of the kingdom of Jerusalem for the Christian conquests was discussed.[34] King Henry II's memorandum of 1311 had also advocated an attack on Egypt. This document is important as the only direct evidence for the opinion of the Cypriot royal family between the fall of Acre and Peter's accession as to how the recovery of the Holy Land might be achieved. Henry recommended a surprise attack on Egypt using Cyprus as a base; even if the Egyptians learnt of the preparations, they would not know where the expedition would strike, and so would have to be ready to defend the whole coast of both Egypt and Syria; furthermore, fear of Mongol incursions would make the Mamluks hesitate to withdraw troops from Syria once the landing had been made; with Egypt secured, the Christians could advance into Syria.[35] Whether Peter knew the contents of his great-uncle's memorandum of half a century earlier is unknown, but both Henry and Peter saw the need for help from the West and both Henry and Peter recognised the advisability of a surprise attack on Egypt. The tradition of thought which regarded this as the best way to win back the kingdom of Jerusalem was thus well established.

We come now to the central problem of Peter's reign: did he, in 1365, expect to be able to restore the Latin kingdom? Peter 'from his youth had desired the liberation of his paternal inheritance, the kingdom of Jerusalem', Philip of Mézières assured his readers.[36] As early as 1362 the king had written to the commune of Florence about his intentions to recover the Holy Land,[37] and Pope Urban repeatedly asserted that the expedition of 1365 was to be 'pro recuperatione Terre Sancte'.[38] (By contrast, Clement VI had consistently described the crusade proclaimed in 1343 as being 'contra Turcos'.)[39] Faced with the testimony of these sources and the circumstantial evidence of the tradition that Egypt was the key to the recovery of Jerusalem, a view allegedly urged by the legate, Peter Thomas, at Alexandria when opposing those who wished to abandon the city,[40] we might incline to agree that Peter genuinely believed he could win back Jerusalem. But it is hard to accept that he really thought he could defeat the Mamluks in Egypt and lead his victorious army into the lands of the former kingdom, or that, having received Palestine in exchange for Alexandria, he could have garrisoned and defended it. Such scepticism finds support when we look more closely at these sources. Philip of Mézières, though an eyewitness, was a crusade-publicist who was obsessed with the idea that Jerusalem should and could be recovered. It was probably he who, as chancellor of Cyprus, had penned the letter to the Florentines. The other principal authorities for the reign, William of Machaut and Leontios Makhairas, refer to Peter's ambition to recover Jerusalem without giving it prominence and without depicting the expedition of 1365 as having that goal.[41] No doubt Peter was prepared to let the pope and Philip of Mézières use the recovery of Jerusalem for propaganda purposes and something of this came to be reflected in the other sources, but it does not necessarily follow that he himself believed his own propagandists.

If the recapture of Jerusalem was not part of Peter's programme in 1365, the question arises of what in fact his policy was. It is clear from the scale of his preparations that he had been planning a major invasion of some part of the Muslim world; he had been absent from Cyprus for nearly three years and during his absence had visited most of the kingdoms of western Europe; he had financed his travels by allowing the Cypriots to buy exemptions for the poll-tax,[42] and when trouble from the Genoese was threatened appears to have conceded all their demands rather than allow them to hinder his schemes.[43] It is also clear that once he had captured Alexandria, he intended to hold on to it.[44] This much is certain. What follows is hypothesis. We have seen that considerations of commerce and security had played a large part in Peter's activities before his visit to the West, and we shall see that the same considerations were to be prominent in the negotiations of the final years of his reign. Let us suggest that Peter's preoccupation in 1362-1365 was similarly not Jerusalem but the interrelated questions of Cypriot trade and defence. Peter knew that if ever the Mamluks or Turks gained control of the sea, Cyprus would be at their mercy. As it was, the most potent naval force in the eastern Mediterranean lay in the hands of the Italian and Catalan merchants. Provided they had a sufficient vested interest in the commercial well-being of Cyprus, the political future seemed assured, for not only would they give aid if the island were threatened, but the revenues from trade in the form of customs and market-dues which accrued to the Cypriot crown would help substantially towards paying for the island's defence. On the other hand, if the merchants stopped trading in Cyprus, not only would the commercial wealth no longer be at the disposal of the authorities, but there would be no assistance should the Muslims mount an invasion.

One of the problems of the 1360s seems to have been that the island's commercial prosperity was threatened and that in consequence the merchants might cease to come in such numbers: Famagusta, the principal port, was handling a declining share of the oriental trade. In the first half of the fourteenth century it had enjoyed immense prosperity based largely upon its role as the chief entrepôt for the spice trade: eastern goods were brought in from northern Syria and Armenia by local middlemen and there sold to western traders. By the end of the century, however, the city was in serious decay, and though the Genoese invasion of the 1370s had aggravated this process, it is almost certain that its chief cause lay in economic factors over which the kings of Cyprus had no control. One of these was the recession which is to be linked with the demographic effects of the Black Death; another was changing trade routes which tended to take the oriental trade with Europe further north through the Black Sea or further south up the Red Sea and through Egypt. Leontios Makhairas rightly saw that among the reasons merchants traded in Famagusta in preference to Syria or Egypt during the period of its greatest commercial prosperity was the papal prohibition on direct trade between Catholics and Muslims;[45] this prohibition had never been totally effective, but there can be no doubt that it had acted as a restraint. From the mid-1340s the papacy was granting increasing numbers of licences to circumvent its own ban on trading in Muslim territories; indeed, in August 1365, while Peter's crusading fleet was waiting at Rhodes, Urban V was issuing yet more licences to the Venetians to trade in Alexandria.[46] There are no statistics to illustrate the extent to which the economic decay of Famagusta had advanced by Peter's reign, but it is not hard to imagine that to contemporary observers Famagusta was in decline because commerce which previously would have been transacted there was now being transacted in Egypt or Syria. If we take the example of the Venetian state-owned galleys which were sent to the East regularly from 1332, such a view would seem to have some degree of validity. From the registers of the Venetian Senate it appears that of the years 1332-1345 in which the republic organised state-galley voyages to the eastern Mediterranean, the usual number equipped was seven or eight and the terminus, after 1334, was invariably Cyprus. In the two decades after 1346, when these galleys first started going to Alexandria, the annual total that sailed for the East remained at around seven or eight, but of these only half were bound for Cyprus; the others were for Egypt. In the years 1357-1359, the eve of Peter's accession, a total of fourteen galleys were equipped for Alexandria and only nine for Cyprus.[47] It must be stressed that we have no way of knowing how far other types of venture or how far other merchant republics followed this change in trading patterns, but, if it was in any way symptomatic of a general trend, the idea that Alexandria was taking trade from Famagusta would be perfectly understandable.

The hypothesis that is proposed is therefore that Peter's war on the Mamluks was aimed at reversing the decline in the share of trade transacted in ports under his control. When he launched his expedition against Alexandria he hoped to achieve one of two things: to capture and hold the city so that in future he and his kingdom would derive profit from its commerce, or if, as indeed it turned out, permanent occupation was not feasible, to destroy Alexandria in the naive expectation that its commercial wealth would revert to Famagusta. It has already been mentioned that Peter intended to hold on to Alexandria, and there is evidence too that it was not until after the decision to withdraw had been reached that a start was made on the systematic destruction of the fortifications.[48] Had Peter been able to keep Alexandria, it would have formed, with Satalia and Gorhigos, one of a series of Levantine ports in Cypriot hands. He would have realised that the capture of Alexandria required a larger force than that with which he had occupied Satalia in 1361; hence the elaborate preparations. Perhaps we might even go so far as to suggest that with Cypriot control of the major ports, Peter might have expected to have such a stranglehold on Egyptian economic life that the long term aim of recovering Jerusalem would not have been quite so unrealistic.

The closing years of Peter's reign were characterised by a complicated series of negotiations. Besides Cyprus and the Mamluk sultanate, Catalan and Italian trading interests were directly involved. The merchants, whose interests had received a major setback by the sack of Alexandria, wanted peace in order to resume their commercial relations with the Muslims, and it was of little importance to them whether or not the settlement favoured the Cypriots. The papacy vacillated: in 1366 Urban was supporting Peter by issuing further crusade indulgences, attempting to prevent negotiations between the Mamluks and the Venetians, banning all trade with the Muslims and calling for the end of a Venetian prohibition on the export of arms to Cyprus;[49] but from 1367 the pope was more willing to follow the demands of the Italians: in 1367 the trading ban was lifted, and, when Peter arrived in Rome the following year, Urban was not prepared to support his request for military help and pressed him to allow the Venetians and Genoese to negotiate a peace on his behalf.[50]

Peter's policy towards the Mamluks after the sack of Alexandria continued to be aggressive. In 1366 he was planning to attack Beirut, the most important port on the coast of Syria, but desisted partly because of Italian pressure and partly, it would seem, because his resources were inadequate.[51] The Venetians had defused Peter's crusade-propaganda in the West by claiming that peace had been made and so dissuaded many of the adventurers who, hearing of Peter's exploits at Alexandria, were preparing to come to the East.[52] If we accept the theory that Peter was fighting a mercantile war, then an attack on Beirut would have been a logical next step after Alexandria, although as the Mamluks were planning a counter-attack[53] Peter could have been thinking more in terms of a pre-emptive assault. At the same time negotiations had opened; according to a document preserved by Philip of Mézières, Peter was demanding the ceding of Jerusalem as the price of peace, but there is reason to suppose that he had no true desire for a settlement and was merely playing for time.[54] Towards the end of 1366 a Cypriot ambassador was imprisoned by the Mamluks; when in January 1367 a large Cypriot fleet belatedly put to sea, it was scattered in a storm, and, though a few ships reached Tripoli where they were reported to have done considerable damage, the expedition as a whole was a failure.[55] It was only after this that serious negotiations for peace were begun, and a settlement would have been reached had not the sultan refused his final ratification.[56] Peter, who had been fully occupied while these negotiations were in progress by a Turkish attack on Gorhigos and a mutiny in the garrison at Satalia,[57] reacted by sending his fleet to raid Tripoli and the ports of northern Syria as far as Ayas.[58] At the close of 1367 Peter set out on his second visit to the West with the expressed intention of raising a further army.[59] No help was forthcoming, and, as has been mentioned, the pope induced Peter to send Venetian and Genoese ambassadors to the Mamluks to sue for peace on his behalf; the embassy reached Cairo in the summer of 1368, but failed to make any progress.[60]

Some idea of what Peter was hoping to achieve in the closing years of his reign can be gained from what is known of the peace negotiations of those years. The text of the treaty of 1367 which, though accepted by the Mamluk emissaries, was not ratified by the sultan has been preserved. Out of the twenty-one clauses the first thirteen are all concerned with commercial franchises for Cypriots and reciprocal trading arrangements. Peter was seeking the same sort of commercial franchises in the Mamluk lands that the Italians had in Cyprus; in particular full rights of jurisdiction over Cypriot merchants and over disputes involving Cypriots and Muslims, and a halving of the customs dues. Other clauses stipulated that the Muslims should not harbour Turks who were making war on Cyprus or pirates, that reprisals were not to be taken on Cypriots for the misdeeds of Christians from the West, and that the king's family and retainers were to have free access to the Holy Places. Two clauses were intended to prevent further conflict by allowing for arbitration and delay in the event of a quarrel, and a final clause indicated that the peace was to include Peter's allies, the Knights of St. John.[61] In the treaty of 1367 there was no reference to the kingdom of Jerusalem, demanded in the negotiations of 1366, but two other demands of that year, customs exemption and the handing over of enemies, reappeared though not necessarily in the same form.[62] In May 1368 Peter agreed to allow the Venetian and Genoese envoys to negotiate on his behalf on the basis of the 1367 treaty. In their instructions they were told to renew the demands for commercial franchises, the customs reductions being given special prominence: if the Mamluks would not agree to a reduction by a half, a third or at least a quarter was to be sought. In addition there was a request for a particular *funduq* in Alexandria for the use of Cypriot merchants. There was also to be a mutual exchange of prisoners and the annual provision for up to fifty members of the royal household to visit the Holy Palaces. The king began his instructions with a clause which stated that any agreement reached was not to be to the prejudice of his rights in Jerusalem, but it is doubtful whether this should be understood as meaning any more than that Peter was not prepared to surrender his titular kingship.[63] The keynote of the negotiations of 1367 and 1368 was thus commerce. Peter was using aggression and the threat of aggression, not to make territorial gains in areas once under Christian rule, but to derive trading advantages at the expense of the Mamluks and, by implication, at the expense of the Cypriots' competitors in the Muslim ports, the merchants from the West.

The remaining history of the war can be briefly told. Between the failure of the 1368 negotiations and Peter's murder in January 1369 no further moves seem to have been made. There were more raids on the Mamluk coast later in 1369 and negotiations were reopened, this time successfully, in 1370. The terms of the settlement are not known, though, if we accept the view that they were similar to those of an agreement of 1403, they were clearly less advantageous to the Cypriots than those of 1367 would have been.[64] Peter was unquestionably a vigorous ruler whose campaigns impressed his contemporaries, but warfare and royal tours of Europe were expensive. He resorted to the expedients of allowing individuals to buy exemption from the poll-tax[65] and of alienating parts of the royal domain to foreign adventurers in his service[66] in his attempts to remain solvent. According to Leontios Makhairas, he had spent all the wealth accumulated by Hugh IV on the expeditions against the Turks before 1362, and by 1366 the king's counsellors were showing concern at the cost to the crown of the military activities.[67] Some indication of the strain caused by the war can be seen in the *remède* issued at the time of Peter's murder: among other complaints the vassals referred to excessive military service, to financial impositions being extended beyond their agreed terminal dates, to the alienation of the royal salt monopoly and to new fiscal burdens imposed against their wishes.[68] There are symptoms too of the increasing difficulties in which Peter found himself in the development of the negotiations of 1367-1368, and there is little doubt that the new regime in 1369 lacked the resources and energy to maintain the former level of pressure on the Mamluks.

Our view of Peter's achievement is clouded by the events of 1373-1374 when the Genoese invaded Cyprus, captured Famagusta and left the kingdom greatly weakened. What he achieved must be considered in the light of what he set out to do. If he had intended to win back Jerusalem, he was a failure; he was also unrealistic. If, as is more likely, he went to war to derive commercial benefits for Cyprus, he may have come nearer his goal, though, being unable to press home his advantage, here too his policy was not crowned with success. Two points should have emerged from this study. Peter's activities were in certain respects a development of earlier policies; his burst of military enterprise should not be seen as an isolated phenomenon but as the continuation of ideas which can be dimly perceived in the quieter and less well-documented reigns of his father and great-uncle. More importantly, the usual view of Peter as the old-fashioned crusader who would win back Jerusalem has been called in question. In its place an assessment of Peter as a political realist with a crude and inadequate understanding of economic forces has been proposed. Thus the capture of Satalia was for reasons of security and trade; the destruction of Alexandria once it was clear that it could not be held could have been an attempt to destroy a rival port to Famagusta; the negotiations of 1367 and 1368 showed commercial franchises as the main Cypriot concern; all the talk of crusade and the recovery of Jerusalem could have been no more than an attempt to supplement Cypriot resources with men and money from the West. This interpretation rests on numerous assumptions, but faced with a choice between Peter, the crusader with delusions of former glories, and Peter, the king who devoted his energies to the struggle for a secure Cyprus protected by its commercial hegemony, the latter has much to recommend it.

PETER W. EDBURY

1. G. Hill, *A History of Cyprus*, Cambridge, 1940-52, II, 368.

2. H. E. Mayer, *The Crusades*, Oxford, 1972, 238.

3. J. Prawer, *The World of the Crusaders*, London, 1972, 148.

4. See in particular, Leontios Makhairas, *Recital concerning the Sweet Land of Cyprus entitled 'Chronicle'* (ed. and trs. R. M. Dawkins), Oxford, 1932, I, paras.116-28, 132-5, 137-44, 150-52, 180, 208, 317-18, 366-9. See also Philip of Mézières, *The Life of Saint Peter Thomas* (ed. J. Smet), Rome, 1954, 96-7; William of Machaut, *La prise d'Alexandrie ou chronique du roi Pierre Ier de Lusignan* (ed. L. de Mas Latrie), Geneva, 1877, 20-21. For the return of Satalia, see Gregory XI, *Lettres secrètes et curiales intéressant les pays autres que la France* (ed. G. Mollat), Paris, 1962-5, no.2198.

5. See Hill, II, 74-5.

6. L. de Mas Latrie, *Histoire de l'île de Chypre sous le regne des princes de la maison de Lusignan*, Paris, 1852-61, II, 216; Benedict XII, *Lettres closes et patentes intéressant les pays autres que la France* (ed. J-M. Vidal and G. Mollat), Paris, 1913-50, no.1673.

7. Leontios Makhairas, I, paras.116-17.

8. P. Lemerle, *L'Émirat d'Aydin, Byzance et l'Occident*, Paris, 1957, 90-100.

9. Lemerle, 181-3, 189-92. For Cypriot contributions to the defence of Smyrna, see *Codice diplomatico del sacro militare ordine gerosolimitano oggi di Malta* (ed. S. Pauli), Lucca, 1733-7, II, 93-4; Mas Latrie, *Histoire*, II, 217-19, 221-2; *Annales ecclesiastici* (ed. C. Baronius and O. Raynaldus, new ed. A. Thiener), Bar-le-Duc/Paris, 1864-83, 1356, para.36; *I libri commemoriali della republica di Venezia regesti (1293-1778)* (ed. R. Predelli and P. Bosmin), Venice, 1876-1914, II, p.264 no.241; Clement VI, *Lettres closes, patentes et curiales se rapportant à la France* (ed. E. Déprez, J. Glénisson and G. Mollat), Paris, 1901-61, nos.2580, 2591, 2749, 2957, 4130, 4661, 5056; Clement VI, *Lettres closes, patentes et curiales intéressant les pays autres que la France* (ed. E. Déprez and G. Mollat), Paris, 1960-61, nos.1079 2377; Innocent VI, *Lettres secrètes et curiales* (ed. P. Gasnau and M-H. Laurent), Paris, 1959- , nos.618, 642, 645, 689, 693, 1630-31, 1788, 1791; Leontios Makhairas, I, paras.114, 119.

10. The Cypriots, however, had Genoese, Hospitaller and Papal assistance. Leontios Makhairas, I, paras.117-19.

11. Liontios Makhairas, I, paras.129, 131, see para.107.

12. *Annales ecclesiastici*, 1360, paras.13-16; Leontios Makhairas, I, paras.102, 105-8. Leontios's dates for this and the embassy of 1361 are impossible. See N. Iorga, *Philippe de Mézières (1327-1405) et la croisade au XIVe siècle*, Paris, 1896, 117 n.4. For the dispute, see Hill, II, 309-10.

13. Leontios Makhairas, I, paras.108-9. See also Mas Latrie, *Histoire*, II, 233, III, 741.

14. Urban V, *Lettres secrètes et curiales se rapportant à la France* (ed. P. Lecacheux and G. Mollat), Paris, 1902-55, nos.119-20. See Leontios Makhairas, I, para.129.

15. Leontios's statement (para.107) that the pope summoned Peter to Avignon in 1360 is directly contradicted by a papal letter of that year. *Annales ecclesiastici*, 1360, para.16. Urban's letters of Nov.1362, though written after Peter had set out, contain no suggestion that he was under summons.

16. *Annales ecclesiastici*, 1363, paras.15-19. See Urban V, *Lettres secrètes*, nos.476-89.

17. Peter's emissary, John of Morf, sent to the West in 1361, had been with King John in Jan. 1362 (1361 o.s.). Mas Latrie, *Histoire*, III, 741.

18. As suggested by A. S. Atiya, *The Crusade in the Later Middle Ages*, London, 1938, 322-3.

19. Mas Latrie, *Histoire*, II, 180-81. See Lemerle, 181.

20. Hugh IV's ambassadors, Peter Le Jaune, Philip L'Aleman and the bishop of Beirut, were at Avignon June-July 1333. John XXII, *Lettres communes* (ed. G. Mollat), Paris, 1904-47, nos. 60648-9; see nos. 60643-7, 60651, 60653, 60655, 60657, 60660-61, 60777-81. The crusade was formally initiated on 26 July. *Op. cit.*, nos. 61202-57.

21. Mas Latrie, *Histoire* II, 118-25 (see paras. 9-11); John XXII, *Lettres secrètes et curiales relatives à la France* (ed. A. Coulon and S. Clémencet), Paris, 1900- , no. 1690.

22. See G. Tabacco, *La casa di Francia nell'azione politica di Papa Giovannii XXII*, Rome, 1953, 63-5, 220-21, 231-2, 235, 303. For the marriage, see Hill, II, 294.

23. Urban V, *Lettres secrètes*, no. 487.

24. See M. Prou, *Étude sur les relations politiques du pape Urbain V avec les rois de France Jean II et Charles V*, Paris, 1888, 27; C. Samaran and G. Mollat, *La Fiscalité pontificale en France au XIVe siècle*, Paris, 1905, 19.

25. Philip of Mézières, *Saint Peter Thomas*, 120-21.

26. For varying estimates, see Philip of Mézières, *Saint Peter Thomas*, 127 see p. 125; Leontios Makhairas, I, paras. 162, 167; 'Chronique d'Amadi', ed. R. de Mas Latrie in *Chroniques d'Amadi et de Strambaldi*, Paris, 1891-3, I, 414.

27. See Hill, II, 329-31. William of Machaut's assertion (pp. 60-63) that Peter was only persuaded to go to Alexandria by Percival of Cologne after he had reached Rhodes seems to have been purely a literary device to flatter Percival.

28. Urban V, *Lettres secrètes*, no. 1703; Leontios Makhairas, I, para. 166.

29. Leontios Makhairas, I, paras. 132-5, 137-44, 150-52.

30. Leontios Makhairas, I, paras. 112-14.

31. Atiya, *Crusade*, 55, 59, 63-4, 80, 105-6, 122, 185.

32. The internal history of Armenia in this period is obscure; the regime seems later to have offered suzerainty to Peter himself. See H. F. Tournebize, *Histoire politique et religieuse de l'Arménie depuis les origines des Arméniens jusqu'à la mort de leur dernier roi (l'an 1393)*, Paris, 1910, 701; Hill, II, 358; W. H. Rüdt-Collenberg, *The Rupenides, Hethumides and Lusignans: The Structure of the Armeno-Cilician Dynasties*, Paris, 1963, p.76 no.196.

33. See R. C. Smail, *Crusading warfare (1097-1193)*, Cambridge, 1956, 22.

34. S. Runciman, *A history of the Crusades*, Cambridge, 1951-4, III, 160-62, 263.

35. Mas Latrie, *Histoire*, II, 118-25. It is not clear whether the Cypriots who presented the memorandum of 1323 (above p.93) held to Henry's views or were prepared to accept Louis of Bourbon's idea of a direct assault on the coast of Syria. See A. B [oislisle], 'Projet de croisade du premier duc de Bourbon', *Annuaire-Bulletin de la Société d'Histoire de France*, IX, 1872, 248-50.

36. Philip of Mézières, *Saint Peter Thomas*, 102.

37. Mas Latrie, *Histoire*, II, 236-7.

38. See for example the bulls cited above n.16.

39. Clement VI, *Lettres closes ... France*, nos.332, 360, 433-4.

40. Philip of Mézières, *Saint Peter Thomas*, 134.

41. William of Machaut, 3, 10; Leontios Makhairas, I, para.131.

42. Leontios Makhairas, I, para.157.

43. For the dispute, see Hill, II, 312-14. For the text of the settlement agreed in April 1365, shortly before Peter's expedition was ready, see Mas Latrie, *Histoire*, II, 254-66. Though Peter was said to have objected to one of the articles in the agreement, he later complied with it. Leontios Makhairas, I, paras.154-5, 173, 174, 209.

44. Philip of Mézières, *Saint Peter Thomas*, 133-4; William of Machaut, 100-109; Leontios Makhairas, I, paras.172-3.

45. Leontios Makhairas, I, para.91.

46. *I libri commemoriali*, III, p.42 no.227; see p.28 no.140, p.43 no.234, p.47 no.267. See W. Heyd, *Histoire du commerce*

du Levant au moyen-âge, Leipzig, 1885-6, II, 45-8.

47. F. Thiriet, *Régestes des délibérations du Sénat de Venice concernant la Romanie*, Paris/The Hague, 1958-61, nos.12, 43, 76, 91, 105, 140, 154, 170, 178, 192, 202, 206, 239, 272, 292, 311, 328, 343, 365, 418, 424, 433, 486, 498. See A. Tenenti and C. Vivanti, 'Le film d'un grand système de navigation: les galères marchandes vénitiennes XIVe-XVIe siècles', *Annales*, XVI, 1961, 83-6.

48. See Atiya, *Crusade*, 367.

49. *Annales ecclesiastici*, 1366, para.16; *Diplomatarium Veneto-Levantinum sive acta et diplomata res Venetas, Graecas atque Levantis illustrantia* (ed. G. M. Thomas and R. Predelli), Venice, 1880-99, II, 110-11, 113-17; *I libri commemoriali*, III, p.51 no.296; Urban V, *Lettres secrètes*, nos.2370, 2416-18.

50. Mas Latrie, *Histoire*, II, 303, 308; *Diplomatarium Veneto-Levantinum*, II, 123-6; William of Machaut, 219-21. Urban was also critical of Peter's behaviour towards his wife and towards Florimond of Lesparre and declined to give him the Golden Rose. *Annales ecclesiastici*, 1367, para.13; Urban V, *Lettres secrètes*, no.2567; Iorga, 374.

51. William of Machaut, 114-22; Leontios Makhairas, I, paras. 177-80.

52. See Hill, II, 335-6, 341.

53. See Hill, II, 337.

54. See Iorga, 321-2; Hill, II, 339-40.

55. Leontios Makhairas, I, paras.185, 189-92.

56. See Hill, II, 344-7.

57. See Hill, II, 348-9.

58. William of Machaut, 204-17; Leontios Makhairas, I, paras.209-12, see para.213. See also *Chronique des Quatre Premiers Valois* (ed. S. Luce), Paris, 1862, 185-91. For evidence that this raid was in retaliation for breaking off negotiations, see Mas Latrie, *Histoire*, II, 292, 304.

59. Mas Latrie, *Histoire*, II, 292; William of Machaut, 219; Leontios Makhairas, I, paras.216-17.

60. See Hill, II, 356-7, 359-60.

61. Mas Latrie, *Histoire*, II, 293-302.

62. See Iorga, 321-2.

63. Mas Latrie, *Histoire*, II, 302-8.

64. See Hill, II, 372-6.

65. Leontios Makhairas, I, paras.157, 215.

66. For example see Mas Latrie, *Histoire*, II, 358-9; *Chypre sous les Lusignans. Documents chypriotes des archives du Vatican (XIVe et XVe siècles)* (ed. J. Richard), Paris, 1962, 80, 84, 91.

67. Leontios Makhairas, I, paras.157, 182.

68. 'Bans et Ordonnances des rois de Chypre, 1286-1362', *Recueil des historiens des croisades. Lois*, II, 378-9. See J. Richard 'La révolution de 1369 dans le royaume de Chypre', *Bibliothèque de l'École des Chartes*, cx, 1952, 110-15.

THE CONTRIBUTORS

P. W. EDBURY graduated at the University of St. Andrews in Mediaeval History in 1970, and received his Ph.D. in 1975 for a thesis entitled *The feudal nobility of Cyprus, 1192-1400*. Since 1973 he has been a Research Lecturer at Christ Church, Oxford.

DUNCAN HALDANE read Arabic and Islamic Studies at the University of Edinburgh, where he obtained his Ph.D. for research on Mamluk painting and manuscripts, gaining access to much material which had hitherto been relatively neglected. At present he is working in Cairo as the Organiser of the B.B.C.'s Middle East Office.

ROSALIND HILL graduated at Oxford (St. Hilda's College). She is a Fellow of the Royal Historical Society and of the Society of Antiquaries. Until her retirement in 1976, she was Professor of History in the University of London. She is the Chairman (and formerly honorary General Editor) of the Canterbury and York Society, and was successively Secretary and President (1974-5) of the Ecclesiastical History Society. Her publications, mainly on medieval ecclesiastical history, include an edition with translation of the *Gesta Francorum*.

P. M. HOLT graduated at Oxford (University College). He is a Fellow of the British Academy. After service in the Sudan, he joined the School of Oriental and African Studies in the University of London, where he is now Professor of the History of the Near and Middle East. He has published on Egyptian and Sudanese history, and is now working on the Mamluk sultanate.

ROBERT IRWIN graduated at Oxford, where he read Modern History, and subsequently carried out research in Middle Eastern History at the School of Oriental and African Studies, London. Since 1972 he has been Lecturer in Mediaeval History at the University of St. Andrews.

JONATHAN RILEY-SMITH graduated at Cambridge (Trinity College). He is at present Lecturer in Medieval History in the University of Cambridge, and a Fellow and Director of Studies in History at Queens' College. His publications include *The Knights of St. John in Jerusalem and Cyprus c. 1050-1310* (1967) and *The feudal nobility and the kingdom of Jerusalem, 1174-1277* (1973).

R. C. SMAIL is a University Lecturer in History at Cambridge, where he is a Fellow of Sidney Sussex College. Among his publications are *Crusading warfare 1097-1193* (1956) and *The crusaders in Syria and the Holy Land* (1973).

INDEX

Wāfidī, Wāfidiyya, 48, 65, 66, 69, 71.
wālī (chief of police), 50, 53, 59.
wālī (governor), 65, 68.
waqf, 72.
wazīr, 49, 51, 57, 58, 64.
William II (king of Sicily), 29.
William of Machaut, 91, 95.
William of Montferrat, 27, 28.
William of Tiberias, 34.
William of Tyre, 1, 3, 32.

Yūsuf, al-Nāṣir, 64, 65, 66.

al-Ẓāhirī, Khalīl, 45, 47, 51, 57.
Zangī (*atabeg*), 54.
Ziada, Mustafa M., 62.